My Great Adventure to Normandy & Back

A WWII Chronicle

Edward P. Kent with Carol L. Rose

iUniverse, Inc.
New York Lincoln Shanghai

My Great Adventure to Normandy & Back
A WWII Chronicle

iUniverse, Inc.

For information address:
iUniverse, Inc.
2021 Pine Lake Road, Suite 100
Lincoln, NE 68512
www.iuniverse.com

ISBN: 0-595-27314-9

Printed in the United States of America

My Great Adventure to Normandy & Back

Best wishes
to Eileen &
Bruce.

Ed Kent 2007

Foreword

My grandfather fought in the Civil War and I always thought it would have been interesting if he had written of his experiences so that the family that came after him would have an insight into that period.

I used to tell my family some of my experiences in World War II and they said that I should write them down. I kept putting it off until my daughter Carol and her husband Jim gave me a small tape recorder for a birthday present and Carol volunteered to transcribe the story.

This is an account of my experiences in World War II. I am not attempting to give a grand overview of the war but to simply tell the story of one young man's adventures while in the service of his country.

Other veterans may read this and say, "it wasn't like that at all." Everyone sees things in a unique and different way and this is the way I saw them. This is a true account to the best of my recollection of the things that happened to me during this part of America's history.

I want to express my thanks to my family for their support and encouragement. A special thanks to Carol and Jim. Without their help this book would never have been written.

Thanks to my daughter Sandy for being my "proof-reader and editor."

Edward P. Kent

My Great Adventure To Normandy & Back

As Told By: Edward P. Kent

June 6, 2000. I choose this date to begin writing my father's memoirs of World War II, especially the D-Day Invasion, fifty-six years later. These are the war stories I grew up hearing over and over. Now it is time to put them into print so that others can experience one World War II Veteran's "Great Adventure".

In May 2000 Dad began recording his memories on tape in Cape May, NJ. He mailed them to me in East Montpelier, VT. We worked this way until September 2002 when the text was finished.

With help from my sister Sandy as the "editor" we finished December 2002.

Carol Lyn Rose (Kent)

1

My great adventure began when I was a young man of eighteen. One Sunday morning I was out in the back yard of my parent's home sawing firewood for the fireplace. I'd been working away for quite a while there when my father came to the back door. He stuck his head out the door and he hollered,

"We're at war!"

I laid the saw down along side of the sawhorse and went into the house to listen to the radio. I never picked that saw up again.

My mother, my dad and myself sat around the radio for most of the day, listening to the reports of the Japanese attack on Pearl Harbor. The date was December 7, 1941.

I had made arrangements with my friend Harry Theis to go out with him that Sunday evening. We wound up at a dance hall, a place called the Dry Dock in Franklinville, and of course everybody was sitting around talking about the "yellow Japanese" and what we ought to do about it.

Harry and I decided the best thing for us to do was to go join the Navy. We decided we'd join the Navy the next morning. We made arrangements for him to pick me up and we'd drive up to Camden in his car.

The next morning my mother came in to wake me up to go to work, I was working at the shipyard at the time. I walked out into the kitchen where my mother was packing my lunch and said,

"Don't bother packing me any lunch today, I'm going to go join the Navy."

Well, mother was flabbergasted to say the least! She didn't think that was a good idea at all. But she saw how determined I was so, I guess we were still discussing it when Harry pulled in the driveway to pick me up.

Harry and I drove up to Camden; we parked the car in Camden and caught a bus to go to Philadelphia, to the Customs House, where the Navy recruiting station was. The place was mobbed; all the patriots were there to join the Navy. So we got our applications from a surly Chief Petty Officer. We filled out our applications and turned them back in. After filling out our applications we handed them back to him and he said with a snarl:

"Go sit down on the bench out there in the hallway and we'll call you in for your physical exam."

They were giving the applicants their physical exams and putting them on the bus and taking them away that very day.

We went out in the hallway and were sitting there on the bench and they kept calling fellas in, but they didn't call us in. The mob kept growing; it didn't seem like it was getting any smaller. So after a while I said to Harry,

"You know it's past lunchtime, why don't we sneak out and go down and get something to eat. Cause it doesn't look like they're going to call us for a while."

So we walked down to Market Street and we were sitting in a diner eating a hamburger and I said to Harry, "You know, I don't feel like going back and waiting in that line. Do you?"

He said, "Nah, let's go join the Army."

We hopped the bus back to Camden, went to the Camden Post Office and looked up the Army recruiting Sergeant. Then we signed up to go in the Army.

One of the stipulations was that we would have to stay together. Of course they'll tell you anything to get you to sign up.

The recruiting sergeant said "Oh yeah, I'll fix it so you stay together, I'll mark it right on your papers."

So of course, being so naive, we believed him. We signed some papers and he gave us more papers to take home to have our parents' sign. We weren't 21 yet we were only 18. We hadn't even registered for the draft, at that time you didn't have to register for the draft until you were 21.

We went home and we both had quite a debate with our parents about getting them to sign. But finally they agreed and signed the papers.

The recruiting sergeant told us we had until Thursday to get our affairs in order, come back, and be prepared to go away. That gave us a couple days to quit our jobs etc.

The next day I went up to the shipyard, got my toolbox out, and quit my job.

I had a '35 Chevrolet that I was still making payments on. I agreed to sell it to a friend of mine, Phillip Kaeferle for ten dollars if he'd pick up the payments. He agreed to do that.

So, I got rid of my car and quit my job. Then said goodbye to my friends. I didn't have any sweetheart to say goodbye to, so that part was easy.

Thursday morning we hopped a bus, we couldn't bring a car because you had to be ready to go away. We hopped a bus and went back up to Camden.

We went in for our physical exam. Of course you have to take all your clothes off and they have a whole bunch of fellas in there for the physical exam. If you have any trace of modesty you lose it quickly in the Army.

I was a little leery about the hearing test because I had always been a little hard of hearing in one ear. I knew I was going to have to bluff it. I got past the hearing test okay; in fact I passed everything fine. Except the last thing they tested us were our hearts. We were all standing in line, everybody stark naked. The medical officer said:

"When I stop in front of you I want you to jump up and down on one foot. I want to listen to your heart."

I was way down near the end of the line and Harry was two or three fellas up nearer the officer. So the doctor would come and stop in front of the recruit and the guy would jump up and down, the doctor would put his stethoscope on the man's chest and listen for a second, pass on and then say,

"Okay, go in the other room and put your clothes on."

They didn't turn anybody down; everybody else was going in and putting their clothes on. Finally it came my turn. Of course I was excited because I really wanted to be accepted. By now Harry was already getting his clothes on.

I jumped up and down and the doctor put his stethoscope on my chest. He listened for a second, moved it around and listened to another place and moved it around and listened to another place. Then he walked around in back of me, put it on my back and listened and finally he said,

"Sorry son, you can't go, you have a heart murmur."

I was very disappointed, very downhearted. I told him, "You don't understand, I _have_ to go. I quit my job, sold my car, said goodbye to all my friends…I just HAVE to go in the Army!"

I kept protesting and finally he said, "Well, look, I'll tell you what. Do you smoke?"

I said, "Yeah, I do".

He said, "Well, you go home and don't smoke, eat lightly, get a good night's rest and come back tomorrow and we'll see if we can't get you in."

Boy, when I was walking down the road to my house I really felt about as low as I ever did in my life. I was just ashamed that I couldn't go away. By this time Harry was already at Fort Dix. That night I didn't smoke any cigarettes ate lightly and tried to get a good night's rest.

The next morning I went back to Camden. The Captain recognized me from the day before and took me aside and said, "Let's listen to your heart again." So he listened, but he still didn't seem satisfied. He said, "Why don't you lie down there for a little while and read the newspaper." There was a bench there so I lay down on the bench and he gave me a newspaper. I was reading the newspaper and he kind of snuck up on me and put the stethoscope on my chest when I wasn't expecting it and he listened for a second and then said, "Okay, you can go!"

2

I got sworn in along with the rest of the fellas. I had to wait around while the rest of them had their physical exam. Then an officer swore us in. But it had taken so long for everybody to get their physical exam and get all their papers squared away and everything that it got to be suppertime; they gave us a meal ticket to go to the Hotel Whitman (named after Walt Whitman) in Camden. We all had our dinner at this hotel and they loaded us on a bus and we went up to Fort Dix. By the time we got up to Fort Dix, as I recall now, it was rather late at night when we pulled in. We couldn't see anything in the pitch-black darkness and everything was strange to us. The Sergeant herded us into a barracks and gave us blankets and sheets to make up the bunks and go to bed.

The next morning we still had our civilian clothes, so when they woke us up we put on our clothes and went down to the mess hall for "chow" they called it. We had our "chow" and then they were marching us down to the buildings where they issue your uniforms.

I guess we were a pretty rag-tag-looking bunch, everybody in their civilian clothes and none of us knew how to march in formation. We were marching down the street and I saw this guy come out on the back porch of one of the barracks we were walking past. He had on blue fatigues and a fatigue hat, a floppy brim hat. This guy was waving, waving, waving at me. It was Harry! I didn't even recognize him in that funny looking outfit.

Of course Harry was a 24-hour veteran by that time! He was in the Army a lot longer than I was.

We went through the usual routine a new recruit goes through. They issue you your uniform and give you all your shots. A couple of the guys passed out when they got their shots. We had indoctrination where they showed us how to wear the uniform. It was quite interesting there at Fort Dix. Of course, nobody knew much about military life. It was a learning process for us all.

Harry and I got together; he was in a barracks not too far from where I was living.

As luck would have it, in about two week's time they were getting people ready to ship out. They didn't do any training at Fort Dix, as it was just a reception center. It was where they received the recruits and then shipped them off to different camps for training. Fortunately Harry and I were both assigned to go to Fort Bragg, North Carolina for the Field Artillery Replacement Training Center. F.A.R.T.C. they called it.

We thought it was great that we were going south for the winter. A small group of us were loaded on a train the next morning and we were off for Fort Bragg.

3

Harry and I were both in the same training battery, as a matter of fact; we had bunks right next to each other in the barracks. We were pretty happy because we were going through this training process together. We found it all very interesting. You had to learn military courtesy, how to wear the uniform and how to recognize the superior officer, the different ranks and ratings and how to address your superiors. We were taught how to do close order drill. We were issued rifles; the old Enfield 303 rifle which was a British leftover from World War I. We trained on the Enfield.

The final part of our training was to go down on the rifle range. That was pretty interesting. Turned out Harry & I were both pretty fair shots, in fact we both shot "sharpshooter". The top score is expert, next is sharpshooter, and then marksman. Because of being a sharpshooter I got to go to BAR school and learn how to fire and field strip the Browning automatic Rifle.

During most of our training at Fort Bragg, Harry and I learned to be cannoneers. They trained us on the Old French 75. That's a 75-millimeter howitzer. We enjoyed learning to load and fire the gun. We had to learn all the different positions that a cannoneer has to serve. It varies at times, but there are roughly seven or eight men on a gun crew of a 75. One is the Chief of Section, usually Sergeant. The second in command is the gunner. And the number one man, two man, three-man etc. The Sergeant passes the sight settings down from the firing officer and gives the command to fire. The gunner adjusts the sights and aims the gun. The number one man pulls the lanyard and fires the gun and the number two man is the loader. All the rest are ammunition handlers and laborers. It's a lot of hard work.

Of course we had to learn all the positions. It was very interesting training, we both liked it. We also trained on the rifle. I had special training on the BAR while Harry went to Radio School.

Later, when I got into my regular outfit, because of my schooling on the BAR I was assigned to be the small arms instructor for my battery. Whenever a new weapon came out that we were going to be issued I would go to school to learn how to fire it and how to take care of it. Then I would come back and instruct the rest of the battery on how to take care of the weapon and fire it. Then I had to take them to the firing range and get everybody qualified.

As the small arms instructor I had a lot of experience with the Thompson sub-machine gun, the BAR, the 45 automatic pistol and the 45 six shooter pistol. I had a chance to do a lot of firing on the range and enjoyed that part of my job. We also had the Springfield rifle and the 30-caliber carbine, which is what we carried into combat.

Another lesson I learned when I was in Fort Bragg occurred on our first pay-day. The lesson was that I was NO gambler! Back in those days, a Private got $21 a month. After we got paid everybody went back to the barracks and a crap game started right a way.

I was standing there watching the fellas shooting crap. I had never even seen a crap game before; I was just a country boy. They were all huddled around this blanket down on the floor, one guy looked up at me and said,

"Come on in and shoot a few".

I said, "I don't know how to play."

He said, "Come on, we'll teach you."

Well, they taught me all right! I lost all my pay and then my watch, which was all that I had to lose; everything else belonged to the Army. I was broke for a whole month. As a matter of fact, I was such a poor gambler that I stayed broke nearly all the time I was in the Army simply from trying to gamble when I shouldn't have. There were only two times when I had any luck, one time down in Florida and the other up in Fort Dix. Other than that my luck was very poor. To this day I don't do very much gambling.

We spent about two or three months training and then we were assigned to our permanent outfits. They were posting up the list of names of people that were going to Pine Camp, New York, the Fourth Armored Division. Harry's name was on the list. I scanned the list and my name wasn't there, so I went in to see the First Sergeant.

"Sergeant, there must be some mistake here. Harry Theis and I we're supposed to stay together. He's going up to Pine Camp, NY and my name isn't on that list. It's on our papers that were supposed to stay together."

I still hadn't learned that what they tell you in the Army and what they do in the Army are two different things. The Sergeant practically threw me out of the orderly room. He didn't want to hear my story.

To add insult to injury, I was put on the baggage detail to load their barracks bags on the train while Harry was boarding the train to go to Pine Camp, NY. I was up there throwing the barracks bags off the truck and onto the train and off he went.

Harry and I didn't meet again until the war was over. He served with the Fourth Armored Division all through the war. They went into action around the Fourth of July, 1944 in France. He fought with them all the way through the war as a machine gunner on a half-track and a radio operator with the forward observer. Both jobs were very, very dangerous. He went through the whole war and never got a scratch.

The Fourth Armored division was the outfit that relived the paratroopers at Bastogne during the Battle of the Bulge. Harry saw a lot of combat; he was a good man.

After Harry had shipped out for Pine Camp I stayed at Fort Bragg for another couple weeks. As a matter of fact they wanted me to stay as part of the cadre and train other recruits when they came in. But I didn't want to do that. I wanted to go to a line outfit and see some action.

4

They assigned me to the Fourth Division, which was stationed in Camp Gordon, Georgia. That was our permanent base for a couple years. Every time I moved in the Army I moved deeper and deeper into the South. It started to get pretty hot in Georgia before our term was over.

At that time it was the Fourth Motorized Division. They had a lot of trucks and everything was motorized, the infantry didn't do much walking, they rode on trucks. It was something new they were trying, it was supposed to be much faster and more efficient. But then, of course when the gas started to tighten up, they cut out the use of the trucks and finally they took the trucks away and it became the Fourth Infantry Division. It remained that way for the rest of the war.

Since we were in the artillery we had truck drawn 105's, 105-millimeter howitzers. They were truck-drawn so we rode in trucks, but we also did a lot of hiking. They wanted to keep us hardened up and trained us to be infantrymen, if necessary.

When I got to the Fourth Division, I arrived there in the middle of the night. After finding the outfit that I was assigned to, which was Battery B 44th Field Artillery Battalion. It was the only regular outfit I ever served in. I stayed right in that outfit until the day I was wounded.

When I found Battery B it was late at night and everyone was in bed asleep, taps had already been played and the camp was quiet. I went to the orderly room and reported to the fellow on duty there, they call him "The Charge of Quarters". I reported to the CQ, he was a real nice guy. He showed me an empty bunk and told me not to worry about getting up for reveille because I had gotten in so late at night. He said,

"When you wake up, go down and get some chow and then report to the Captain."

I heard the bugle in the morning and just turned over and went back to sleep. About 8 or 9 o'clock I got up and went down the mess hall. The cooks were real nice; they really made me feel at home. Everybody in the outfit was very receptive. I was the only recruit that came in that time, usually they came in three or four, or maybe ten at a time. But this time I came in by myself and everyone made me feel like I had arrived where I belonged.

Edward P. Kent
AGE 19
Camp Gordon, Georgia—1943

I reported to the Captain and he assigned me to the fourth gun section. In the artillery the batteries are divided into sections. In a firing battery, that is a battery that does the firing, they have the gun section, the machine gun section, the wire section, the motor section and the radio operators. I stayed in that Fourth Gun Section the whole time I was in the outfit.

This was where the training got serious. In Fort Bragg it was just basic training, but when you get into your regular outfit you get into serious training. We would go off on bivouacs and field problems and tactical field problems where you are training in combat conditions. As close to combat conditions as they could make it. Everything was blacked out and we'd have motor marches under strict black out restrictions.

It was a lot of hard work, especially in the gun sections, it seemed to me. A lot of our work was lugging ammunition around and the ammunition was pretty heavy. We had truck drawn guns and had to manhandle them around, unhooking them from the truck and getting them into position. I was on the 105 Howitzer; it was more or less the basic artillery piece of the armed services. To this day it still is.

An amusing thing happened when we were in Camp Gordon. It seems that our Captain was pretty lenient with fellas who came in an hour or two late off of furlough. He figured they had to make a lot of connections with buses and trains etc. and if you were an hour or two late he wouldn't say anything.

Headquarters must have cracked down on him; because one night at retreat he made the announcement that from now on, we had to be back in camp on time. He wasn't going to take any more excuses about missing a bus or anything like that. He was really going to crack down.

We were stationed right near Augusta, GA and we had to catch a bus from Augusta to Columbia, S.C. and there catch a train called the Silver Meteor, which ran all the way up through Philadelphia and New York City.

This one fella went on furlough, I believe he lived in NY. This is the story he told us about his trip back from his furlough:

He was on the Silver Meteor and it was in the middle of the night. He was really dog-tired. He'd been doing a lot of "playing around" on his furlough. He thought he'd take a little nap, so he asked the soldier next to him if he was getting off at Columbia.

The guy said, "Yeah, I'm getting off at Columbia."

So my friend said,

Wake me up when we get to Columbia, I want to get a little rest."

So he fell asleep, I guess it was maybe three or four o'clock in the morning when he woke up with a start. The train was stopped and the fella next to him wasn't in his seat. He figured they had gotten into Columbia and the other soldier had forgotten to wake him up! So he grabbed his barracks bag, ran down to the end of the car and jumped off the train. By this time the train was starting up. The train pulled out and he looks around and he is way out in the middle of nowhere. The train must have stopped to get water and the fella next to him must have gotten up to use the men's room or something. He'd jumped off the train and he was out in the middle of the woods and he had no idea where he was!

North Carolina is a very big state and there is a lot of wilderness and he must have been right in the middle of it. He started walking along the tracks, he figured if he headed in the direction the train was going he would come to a town sooner or later.

Well, he walked and walked and finally day broke and he was still out in the wilderness. After a while he came upon a little town. By this time it was 9 or 10 o'clock in the morning. First thing he did was find a Western Union Telegraph Office and he sent a telegram to our Battery Commander explaining that he'd got off the train accidentally, but he would get into camp as soon as he could. He was supposed to be in camp by reveille that morning.

Finally, he caught a hop on a truck and the guy took him to Columbia S.C. and he caught the bus into Augusta. About four o'clock in the afternoon he walked down our Battery Street and went into the orderly room to report to the Captain. Well, the Captain was hot!

He said, "Didn't you pay attention when I said that I wasn't going to listen to any more excuses?"

The soldier explained the situation to him and said, "Didn't you get my telegram?"

The Captain said, "No, I didn't get any telegram. That's a cock and bull story you're feeding me!"

He said, "No, honest sir. I did send you a telegram."

The Captain said, "Alright, if that telegram comes you'll be okay; I won't give you any extra duty. But if I don't get that telegram you're in deep trouble!"

Sure enough, the next day the telegram came and the guy got off the hook. But when the story got around the Battery, everyone had a big laugh about it.

5

At this time the war wasn't going too well for us. In North Africa the allies were being pushed back here and there. Our division got put on "red alert". That meant we were liable to be shipped out at any time. The rumor was around that we were heading for the desert. We packed up all our gear and loaded the guns on the flat cars.

Of course in the Army it's hurry up and wait all the time. We worked like mad but the word never came down for us to pull out. Three or four days went by, we were all sitting on the edge of our chairs, very anxious, wondering what was going to happen. Rumors were flying thick and fast. Finally, the word came down, we were pulling out.

Everybody got all their gear packed into their barracks bags and they marched us down to the train. They had a railroad siding that came right into the camp. We were all lined up along side of the train, waiting to board the train, heading for what we thought was North Africa. The order came down, "Go back to the barracks, it's been called off."

I don't know whether it was a dry run or they just had a final change of plans. We thought we were going to go overseas right away and it didn't happen.

However, a short timer later they did take about half of our battery and sent them to North Africa for replacements.

The gunner on the fourth gun section, Jim Hall, was a good friend of mine that had taught me how to be gunner, how to work the sight. It's a bit complicated with math to do. You have to do it all in your head, doing it quickly and you have to do it sometimes under fire, under stress. It was a very interesting job and that's what I aspired to be, a gunner. Jim Hall was in the group that went to North Africa. I never did find out what happened to him.

I was made the gunner and given a promotion to Corporal. I stayed a gunner for the duration of the war. I really enjoyed that job. It was an important job to do, because the gunner was the one that aimed the gun. Most of the time it was indirect fire, the executive officer was given the compass readings and he would lay the battery to point in a certain direction of the compass. All four guns had to be laid, they had to all be parallel no matter where you were in relation to the other guns, you had to be firing parallel to all the other guns.

The Executive Officer would give us the readings that we would set it off on our sight. Everything was in millimeters; of course millimeters were strange to all of us at the time. After we would get the guns laid, we would put out our aiming stakes. You set one aiming stake about 25 feet from the gun and the other one about 50 feet from the gun. You had to line them up in the sight; the sight had cross hairs on it. You'd use that as a reference point every time they'd give you a change of command, a change of deflection. It might say "right 3 zero" that would mean you'd subtract three zero from whatever reading was set on the sight. That would move the head of the sight 30 millimeters to the left. Then you would traverse the gun until you came back on the aiming stakes, you had to have it lined up right on the aiming stakes. That of course would shift the fire.

This had to be accurate because if you made a mistake in your settings on the sight you wouldn't be firing on the target; you'd be off the target and sometimes firing on your own troops. It was very important that you keep track exactly on what you were doing, you had to pay particular attention, had to concentrate on the job.

After the false start of our supposed deployment overseas, it settled back into the routine of training. We had field problems and a lot of hiking. They started us off with ten mile hikes, then up to fifteen, twenty and twenty-five mile hikes. The longest one I recall was thirty-three miles. When you're walking thirty-three miles in that hot Georgia sunshine with a steel helmet on your head, a rifle on your shoulder and a pack on your back, gas mask and of course all this equipment rubs and chafes. It got very uncomfortable after a while; you get tired and your feet get sore.

I was always proud of the fact that I never fell out on a march. I always finished every march we started out on. A lot of the fellas would get tired, get a blister or something and they'd fall out. An ambulance followed the column and the medics in the ambulance would pick them up and treat their feet if they were blistered. If they had heat exhaustion they would put them in the ambulance and let them ride for a while and cool down. It was good training as it hardened us up.

6

After a few months of this it was wintertime again. The artillery got their orders to deploy to Fort Sill, Oklahoma. We were going to go out there and fire for the Officers Candidate School. So we loaded our guns on flat cars and we got on this train going out to Fort Sill. We were really riding in style this time, we had compartments, and my section had compartments anyway.

Of course a troop train, unless they were really in a hurry, would get diverted for every freight and passenger train because all they were doing was moving us from one fort to another, so it wasn't any priority. We were about three to five days on this train.

We were going through Missouri and had stopped to take on water, there was a steam engine pulling the train. We were way out in the sticks somewhere in Missouri. We were all hanging out the windows, taking in what scenery there was.

A kid came walking along side of the train and he looked up and said, "Would you soldiers like to have some moonshine?"

The guys all hollered, "Yeah! How much is it?"

He said, "A dollar a bottle."

We were just about broke, with not much money at all. So we scrounged around and took up a collection and between our gun section we managed to get up a dollar in change. We said, "Yeah, go get us a bottle."

So he goes off over this little hill. We sat there and sat there, after a while the train whistle blew and the train started up real slow. Just about that time the kid ran back over the hill with a bottle in his hand. It was a 7UP bottle with a white cap on it. He's running along side of the train holding up the bottle saying, "Give me the money. Give me the money."

I was holding the money in my hand and said, "Give me the bottle."

We simultaneously made the transfer, I handed him the money and he handed me the bottle. By this time the train was picking up speed and he fell behind.

We sat there looking at this 7UP bottle; the cap was painted, it looked like it had a different cap on it. We got out the belt buckle; we used to open bottles with our belt buckles. I was opening up this bottle and I heard it go Pssssh. I never realized that moonshine was carbonated! We took a taste of it and it was good old 7UP! That kid had sold us a bottle of 7UP, which sold in those days for a nickel, for a dollar! All he did was paint the cap. I guess that kid must have done that for every troop train that stopped for water. I told the guys that by the end of the war that guy would own half of Missouri!

We arrived in Fort Sill. At that time they had a pack artillery outfit where they carried the cannon on mule backs. They had these small 75's that they would take apart and have a pack train. It would take three or four mules to carry one gun. We used to watch them leading those mules around.

Fort Sill Oklahoma was kind of a dreary place. It was very flat. In the distance we could see some hills or mountains. We never had any field problems; we were only there to fire the cannon for Officers Candidate School.

This is where they trained the artillery officers to be forward observers. These are the eyes of the artillery. They're out forward with the front line troops and they call down the fire of the artillery on the different targets that they spot. It's a very dangerous job because they are right up front when they're in combat. It's also a very demanding job because they have to be as accurate as possible without wasting too much ammunition getting the guns to fire right on whatever target they pick out.

When the forward observer would spot a target, for instance, a machine gun nest, he would look at it with the binoculars and range finder and that would give him an idea how far off the target was. He would then look up the coordinates of the target on his map and either radio or telephone back to the firing battery that information. A radio or telephone operator is working with the forward observer all the time. They'll call back to their battery and have one gun fire a round and it's kind of a guess where it's going to go. They'll give them the deflection and the range and this gun will fire a round and they can spot wherever it bursts. They can spot it with their binoculars. If it bursts over the target or to the left of the target they have to estimate how much to bring the gun back to the right and how much to drop the elevation so that the next round will be on or near the target.

Actually, what they try for is if they can get an "over" and a "short" they kind of average it out between the two and that next round should be right on the target. This is their job and they have to be trained to do this and Fort Sill, Oklahoma was the place where they did this training.

After they get the gun firing on or relatively close to the target, then they'd radio back to their battery and have them fire all four guns. If it is a big target they'll fire a whole battalion of guns, of course there's three firing batteries in the battalion so there would be twelve guns firing on the same target if it is a large installation. It's pretty impressive when they have the fire coming in from twelve guns. Sometimes they fire three rounds or five rounds from each gun. That's a lot of high explosives going out there.

Our job was to actually fire so they could practice adjusting the fire. As I recall, we never unloaded our own guns off of the flat cars. They gave us 75 milli-meters to fire because they had a lot of 75-millimeter ammunition left over from World War I. They were using that up in firing for the OCS school.

The 75's were a little bit smaller artillery pieces than ours were. They had a fixed round of ammunition that was just like a rifle bullet, it didn't come apart. Our ammunition came apart, you had to cut the powder bags etc., and you didn't do this with a 75. You just threw this round in there and fired away.

We had a lot of fun; we did a lot of firing. We'd take turns loading and some-times we'd be firing ten or twelve rounds in succession, we would just throw them in the breech block, pull the lanyard and fire them off as fast as we could.

It was a lot of hard work. We were out in the field all day, every day. It was winter and was cold. When we got out there they put us up in squad tents, a pyr-amid tent that will hold eight to ten men. These tents were winterized tents. They were built on a wooden platform and had a stove, a wood stove in the cen-ter of the tent with the stovepipe going out through the top of the pyramid.

Sometimes on a real cold day, or a real cold night we'd get these stoves fired up. Man, they'd be glowing red, red hot. Of course your back would freeze and your front would be burnt up hanging around this stove trying to get warm.

We had quite a few tents burn down because the hot embers would be blow-ing out the stovepipes and falling on other tents and they'd catch fire. We lost a lot of tents that way.

It was just a bit rugged because it was so cold. We had a washhouse, not a reg-ular barracks with a latrine where we could wash up.

This washhouse was just outside, like a shed. It had barrels of water in there; you'd dip the water out of the barrels into your steel helmet. That's what you would wash and shave in. You'd have to shave with cold water. I can remember many a morning I'd get down there and have to take my steel helmet and break the ice on top of the wash barrel to get the water to wash up. It was a bit primi-tive, but a good experience for us.

As I said before, the countryside was pretty desolate, very flat. One interesting thing was to see all the oilrigs pumping away. There were oilrigs everywhere. We came through, I guess it was Oklahoma City, they had these oilrigs right in the middle of the city. They were all pumping oil, the big wheel going around and the boom going up and down. It looked strange to us to see these oil pumps right in the city. Of course they were scattered all over the countryside.

I think I only went into town one time. The nearest town was Lawton; it wasn't much of a town. It was strictly a soldier town. There wasn't much to do, standing around on the corner and watch the traffic go by. Most of the time I stayed in camp.

I guess we were out in Oklahoma about a month or so. Finally we got our orders to pack back up and were going back to Camp Gordon. We got all packed up and loaded back on the train. This time I didn't ride in the compartment. I pulled the Corporal of the Guard.

It seems we had a guard detail on our guns that were on the flat cars. Of course at that time in the middle of the war, everybody was afraid of saboteurs

We had to guard all our equipment to keep anybody from committing sabotage on it. There were two guards on each flatcar. I think we had two guns on each flatcar that would give us two flatcars. I had a detail of about 4 to 6 guards that I was in charge of.

These poor guys had to ride on the flatcars and it was cold going back. When the train stopped, which it did quite often, they'd have to jump down. One guy would jump down off one side of the car and the other guard would jump off the other. They would march up and down with their rifles guarding this flatcar with our guns on it.

I was riding in the caboose; I was lucky riding with the brakeman. We had a stove in there. Of course every time the train stopped I had to go out and check on my guard detail, make sure everybody was okay and everything was going smooth.

If one of the guys was sick, I would let him ride in the caboose and I would take his place. Most of the time I rode in the caboose. It was something different; it was an interesting trip.

After about three or four days on the train we arrived back at our camp. It was like coming home after being away on an extended trip. We were back in our original barracks with our original gang.

7

We settled down to our regular training routine of marches, bivouacs and firing problems. We'd go out on the range and fire small arms. They tried to keep us up with the latest news of how the war was going and we were getting all the latest equipment.

The major piece of new equipment we got about this time was our tanks. We called them tanks; but they weren't really tanks, they were self-propelled artillery. It was a tank chassis with no turret, just an open top, mounted inside this tank chassis was a 105-millimeter howitzer, which was our main armament. The tank also had a ring turret on which there was a 50-caliber machine gun, which was our secondary armament.

Boy, we were tickled to death with these new tanks. We thought they were great. We could ride in the tank, instead of riding in a truck and towing the gun. When we pulled into position we just had this one vehicle to pull in position and get it pointed in the right direction. There was no gun to unhook and push around. It made it a lot faster; we could pull into position and start firing immediately.

With the truck drawn guns you had to unhook the gun from the truck and swing it around and get it pointed in the right direction. It had what was called a split trail, we had to split the trails and prepare for action. That was one of our commands, "Prepare for action." That meant, get your ammunition out, get the gun laid and get ready to commence firing.

The one disadvantage that these tanks had was the traverse on the 105 was only about 60-65 degrees. Whereas with a tank with a turret, the turret can rotate all the way around and you can fire in any direction. We couldn't fire in any direction; we could just fire to the front. If a target came up that was to right flank, the left flank or to the rear we have to start up the tank and turn the tank around and point it in the direction that the target was going to be. Other than that they worked out real well.

It was quite an experience riding on one. I remember the first time that I rode in ours, of course we ran it down the road. They ran about 35 miles an hour; you could go anywhere with them, within reason. You could go cross-country and it was almost like riding in a boat, the way it would go up and over obstacles.

Our tanks were powered by a rotary airplane engine; the engine was mounted in the back in an armored compartment in the back end of the tank. The driver sat down below the level of our gun deck. The Sergeant or the Corporal, whoever was directing the tank at that time would actually direct it, the driver just followed our command.

Our position was right in back of the driver. When we stood up his shoulders were just about to our knees or almost waist level. If we wanted him to turn right we would pull on his right shoulder and he in turn would pull on the right lever, which would lock the track on that side and the tank would swing around to the right. The harder we'd pull back on his shoulder, the harder he'd pull back on the lever and the tighter the turn. We more or less directed the driver he followed our commands. His vision was somewhat limited as he had to look out a little window, if we were under fire we'd drop a lid down and then he had a little slot to look out. There was bullet-proof glass over the slot, and he had to look out there. His vision was very limited. He had to depend on us to direct him and tell him where to drive.

All the men in the gun section had to learn how to drive the tank, It was a lot of fun learning to drive the thing. It had an accelerator and a clutch, no brake pedal, a tachometer to tell you how many revolutions the engine was turning. Instead of a steering wheel it had two levers, they were the brakes, if you were running along and you wanted to stop you'd just pull back on both of the levers at the same time. If you wanted to turn right, you'd pull back on the right hand lever and it would brake the right track and the tank would swing around to the right. It was the same way with the left.

The tank would go about 35 mph on the highway. It had rubber treads, two endless tracks, one on each side, We could go cross-country and down over the creeks and shallow rivers. We could go through 3 or 4 feet of water without any problem.

When we made the landing on D-Day, we had waterproofed the tank and we could run through 6-8 feet of water, that of course was a special occasion. We had some special equipment on it; one that was called a snorkel. It was a big sheet metal affair that was rigged up on the air intake on the back deck of the tank. This thing looked like air conditioning pipe, it was a big thing. It had a curve at the top that deflected the exhaust down so that we could run through 6-8 feet of water without water getting into the engine and stalling the engine out. We had to waterproof every rivet on the outside of the tank. The tanks were riveted together; there were more rivets than there was welding in those days. We had this real heavy, sticky stuff and we had to crawl underneath the tank and get this stuff smeared around every rivet. We'd run the tank through a pool and check it out for leaks.

This was all in preparation for the D-Day landing; we did all this over in England.

So after our honeymoon with our new tanks, we settled back to our regular training. Part of it was learning to fire every conceivable weapon. We learned how to fire the bazookas, we had a couple of bazookas in the battery. We also learned to fire rifle grenades, light and heavy machine guns; our battery was armed with 50 caliber machine guns. Even though we weren't in the machine gun section, we had to know how to fire them in case we had to use the weapon at any time.

We learned how to throw hand grenades. They even showed us the German hand grenades, the German "potato masher". We learned one very interesting thing at that time; these potato mashers have what looks like a condensed milk can on the end of a stick, a wooden handle. At the end of the wooden handle they have a little screw cap. In order to prepare the thing to throw, you had to arm it, you'd hold the handle with one hand with the other hand you unscrew this little cap and pull it. There was a wire attached to this cap, when you pulled the wire it would start a powder train burning and you had just so many seconds to get rid of the grenade.

In our grenades, you'd pull the pin, there was lever that fit in the palm of your hand and when you threw it, that lever would automatically fall off and start the powder train burning.

With the German grenades, you'd pull the little cap. They taught us to be very careful if you pick up a German hand grenade that there is not a red dot on the cap. They would paint a dot of red paint on some of these grenades. If you took one of those and unscrewed the cap and pulled it, it was good-bye. There was no time delay at all, these were booby traps that would go off and kill you instantly! That was good thing to remember. I never had an occasion to throw a potato masher. I've seen a lot of them and sure enough some of them did have a little dot of red paint on the cap. They told us what to look for.

They taught us mine detection and how to disarm mines. In fact, I went to Mine and Demolition School and then I had to come back and teach the rest of the battery what I had learned about mines and demolition. I was supposed to be the "mine man" for the battery. I never had too much of an occasion to work with them. But it was something good to know.

We also learned how to fire mortars, which are basically an infantry weapon. We had to know how to fire everything in case you had to use it. In fact, we even learned how to load and fire the anti-tank gun. We had two types, the 57-mm and the 37-mm. The thirty-sevens were being phased out because they were so light. The fifty-seven was the weapon used mostly in combat.

We had an interesting time, a lot of time out in the field. Sleeping on the ground in pup tents, eating out of a mess kit. We were getting to be old soldiers by this time. It was a well-trained outfit

After all of this training we got our orders that we were going to make a move. We were going to, of all places, Fort Dix, which was only about forty-five or fifty miles from my home. I thought that was great.

8

We were leaving Camp Gordon, our home camp. We had been there a couple years. Our base camp was now going to be Fort Dix. Our whole division moved to Fort Dix, we had a good time up there.

Of course we continued with the same kind of training. One time we pulled a motor march, the whole division all the way down to Avalon from Fort Dix. We bivouacked in the marsh in back of Avalon. And boy, the mosquitoes and green head flies just about ate us up! We were down there about three or four days. Then they gave us a day off, I think it was a Sunday. They trucked us to the beach in Avalon. Some of the fellas I was in the Army with had never seen the ocean before. It was amusing to see them. They just couldn't get over all that water out there, the beach and everything. They were all laying around in their bathing suits; those that had bathing suits, the others just rolled up their pant legs and took off their shirts. I told them

"You know you'd better watch yourself, you're going to get sunburn. This salt air and sun will really burn you."

They said, "Ah, no. We're used to this. We've worked out on the farm, out in the cotton fields and the tobacco fields all day long with our shirts off."

I said, "Yeah, but this salt air's different."

Sure enough, the next day a lot of them couldn't even put their shirts on. Of course in the Army if you get sunburned so badly that you can't pull duty you'd get court-martialed and given extra duty. You're not supposed to do things that will prevent you from doing your regular duty. It was quite an experience for the fellas from the south. Places like Alabama, Mississippi, they had never seen the ocean before.

Here is one amusing incident that happened in Camp Gordon when we were getting ready to make our move to Fort Dix. I was put in charge of a detail to go down to the railroad siding and clean up a boxcar and get our kitchen installed in this boxcar. Whenever we made a move on a troop train we did our own cooking right on the train. In a boxcar they'd set up a frame and put sand in this frame and then put the stoves in on top of this sand. The cooks would then have a "kitchen car". The boxcar was big enough that the mess Sergeant could put all his equipment in there and he could cook meals for the whole battery.

24

This old boxcar was down on the siding and it had to be cleaned up and have the kitchen put in. I was given about four or five men to go and clean it up. It was an after-duty thing, I remember it was nighttime and we were pushed for time. We had a time deadline to get this boxcar ready for the move to Fort Dix. We were working down there at night. They had sentries walking up and down alongside the train to guard the train, making sure nobody planted a bomb on it. Everybody was still on edge about saboteurs.

We were working away in this boxcar; it was a filthy thing. We had buckets of water and were washing it down. We were just about finished; I grabbed a bucket of the dirty water. It was the dirtiest water you ever saw.

We had the sliding door open; I walked over to the open door and threw the bucket of water out, it was so dark I didn't see the sentry and it splashed all over the sentry! Man was he hot! Of course I didn't mean to do it. I was apologizing, but we were all laughing and he thought we'd meant to do it. He wanted me to fight, but we finally got him calmed down.

Let me tell you a little bit about guard duty. Guard duty came around every so often and was required. I was a Corporal, so I pulled the Corporal of the Guard. When you're on guard duty everybody considers it an honor because you are guarding your comrades while they are sleeping. When you were ordered to go on guard duty you'd make sure your shoes were polished until they'd shine like mirrors and made sure all your web equipment was sparkling clean and your rifle was spotless. You'd just have to be as near perfect a soldier as you could be. The Officer of the Guard inspects you. It's a very demanding inspection. If you get thrown off the guard detail, for a dirty rifle for example, it's a black mark against you. You don't ever want to do that. You want to be at your best on the guard detail.

They have three guard details, three Corporals and a Sergeant. Each Corporal has enough men to cover the post. The post could range anywhere from one or two posts to half a dozen to a dozen. They are all numbered. Post number one was right around the guardhouse, there is always a sentry walking around the guardhouse. Post-number two was a certain area and perhaps post-number four would be the motor park. They always have a guard at the motor park; he'd walk around the trunks and tanks that were parked.

Each Corporal has to know where all these posts are because if one of the fellas has a problem, he'll call out: "Corporal of the Guard, post number three." The fella on post # 2 would relay it until word got back to the Guardhouse. The guard walking around the guardhouse would stick his head in the door and say, "Corporal of the Guard, post number three."

So the Corporal would know to go down to post number three and find out what the problem was. It could be anything. The guy could have seen something suspicious, or he might just have to go to the bathroom. Sometimes the Officer of the Guard, usually a Lieutenant, would decide maybe three or four o'clock in the morning that he was going to go out and surprise these guards. Some of these Lieutenants would sneak up on a guard and try to scare them.

Of course, everybody is armed but this is one time when your rifle was loaded. When you were on guard duty you had live rounds in your rifle, you were ready for trouble, if it so happened.

We'd be two hours on duty and four hours off. When it was nearly time to relieve the guard I would line up my guard detail and inspect them and be sure everybody knew their general orders. We'd march down to the post and relieve the guard on post number one. He would challenge us, and say "Halt, who's there?"

I'd say, "Corporal of the Guard."

Then he'd say, "Advance to be recognized."

We'd march up and he'd recognize us and then they'd switch. I would see that he unloaded his rifle and gave the ammunition to the fella that was going to relieve him. He would load his rifle and I had to supervise the loading of his rifle. I had to make sure he had all of the rounds under the bolt and the rifle on safety and locked. The fella that I had relieved would fall in at the end of our column and we'd march around and relieve all the guards one right after the other.

After you get them relieved you got back to the guardhouse and these fellas that were relieved were off for four hours. They could sleep or read or write letters, but had to stay around the guardhouse. There was one other guy there in the guardhouse, the bugler. The Corporal of Guard had to wake the bugler up.

When you hear that song, "Oh, how I hate to get up in the morning." About how the guy was going to get the pup that has to wake the bugler up, well that was me, the Corporal of the Guard!

One instance that happened about one or two o'clock in the morning when I had posted the guards and relieved the others and they were all back in the guardhouse asleep. I had a little desk in the guardhouse right by the door. I was sitting at this desk; just about half dozed off as it had been a long day. The guy on number one post that was walking around the guardhouse came to the back step of the guardhouse; put his foot up on the step, put the muzzle of his rifle on top of his foot and pulled the trigger. Well man, when that rifle went off I must have jumped five feet into the air! It was only about ten feet from where I was sitting and everything was so quiet. Of course it woke everyone up and we ran out and there was this guy standing there looking at the hole in his shoe.

I had to put a guard to take his place and then we rushed him over to the infirmary. They rushed him off to the hospital and I never saw him again. It was a self-inflicted wound; I guess he got tired of the Army. This happened every once in a while, but it was quite surprising to me. That was the most exciting thing that ever happened to me when I was on guard detail.

Other times when we'd be on guard detail they would send one squad over to the stockade. This was just every so often, maybe once every two months. The whole battalion would share these chores. You had to over to the stockade and chase prisoners. The prisoners in the stockade were guys who had gone over the hill, deserted, or some of them were in for crimes a lot worse than that. Some had knifed people in a fight or something like that. They had some pretty bad guys there.

They would turn these fellas loose with a guard and they would go out and pick up papers and do odd jobs around the place. The guard had to chase them around, that's why they called them "prison chasers".

One thing they always used to tell us that to this day I don't know if it was a myth or an actual fact. They said, if you were chasing a prisoner and he got away you had to pull the balance of his time. Whenever I was on that detail I was determined no prisoner was going to get away. I wasn't going to be pulling any time in the stockade! I'd made up my mind to that.

That stockade is one nasty place. When a fella goes in the stockade and comes out, he's never the same. If you remember seeing the movie "From Here to Eternity" when Frank Sinatra got thrown in the stockade. It's true man; they were really rough!

We had a fella by the name of Brown; we called him Brownie. He was in my gun section for while. He was a pretty good soldier but he had a drinking problem. He didn't drink because he liked the taste of it or anything. He just drank because he wanted to get drunk.

When they put him on KP they had an awful problem with him drinking up all the vanilla extract. He would just get bombed out of his mind.

When we arrived up at Fort Dix he got an overnight pass to go into New York City. In New York City he was sitting in a bar drinking and he started telling the guys in the bar all about these new tanks that we got, the M-7's. It seems there were a couple of guys from the FBI in this bar and they overheard him. They picked him up and he was court-martialed for disclosing military secrets. He got six months in the stockade.

After the six months was up he came back to the outfit. I asked him one time, "What was it like in there Brownie?"

He said, "Man you don't want to know. Just stay out of that place."

Before he went in he was kind of a happy-go-lucky guy when he was sober. But when he got out his personality was changed. He was very withdrawn and sullen with a hair trigger temper. It really changed him. So I made up my mind that I was going to stay out of that place.

9

I'd like to tell you about a few of the fellas that were in my outfit.

My Sergeant's name was Ruben Breland; he was the nicest guy. He was very quiet, almost gentle. I served in the outfit for three years and I never remember him speaking harshly to anybody. He was certainly not the type of guy you'd picture as a Sergeant. But he made a good Chief of Section. He was my immediate superior; between the two of us we ran the fourth gun section. He was from Louisiana, a Cajun.

When the order came down that the Chiefs of Sections were allowed to name their vehicles he named our tank "Catahula" after Lake Catahula in Louisiana. He was from that section of the country. I think he had been a commercial fisherman.

When we were shipping out of Camp Gordon for the final time moving up to Fort Dix, somehow or other they allowed civilians into the camp if they knew someone that was moving out. Some of the officers had their wives there. Breland, we called him the Greek, I don't know why. He wasn't Greek, but I guess he looked like one.

Well, the Greek had this girlfriend. We didn't even know he had a girlfriend until that time. She came in to see him off. We were all formed up marching out of the battery area down to the railroad siding to get on the train. It was just like a scene out of the movies about the Foreign Legion, where the soldiers were marching off and the women were running alongside, hanging around their necks and kissing them good-bye. It was kind of funny, but it was sad too because I don't think she ever saw him again. He died much too young.

Another man that I greatly admired was a fella named Fred Paddock. He was from Florida, West Palm Beach, I believe. When I first joined the outfit he was a Lieutenant. Executive Officer of the battery. Shortly after that our Battery Commander got transferred to another outfit and they gave Lieutenant Paddock a promotion and he became Captain Paddock. He was our Battery Commander for the rest of the time I was in the outfit.

Captain Paddock was a professional soldier, a good man. The men would follow him anywhere and do whatever he said. It was a privilege to serve under someone like him. He was very intelligent and very military. He was one of the bravest men I've ever seen.

One time when we were over in Normandy moving into a new gun position, we had to pull the tanks into this open field between the hedgerows and commence firing immediately. We had a high priority target to commence firing on. We did not have time for the engineers to sweep the field to make sure there weren't any anti-tank mines in this field. Captain Paddock had sandbags on the floor of his jeep. He told his driver to get out; he would drive the jeep himself. He drove back and forth across this field one-way and then back and forth in the opposite direction.

In other words he'd tried to cover every possible inch of that field. If there had been any mines in that field, his jeep would have set them off. As soon as he got through running back and forth across this field he said,

"Okay, move them in."

So we pulled into the field and set up our guns in position and started firing. This was just one instance of the kind of things he would do. Unfortunately, he had a sad thing happen after I had left the outfit. He was out riding around in his jeep with a driver and a radio operator with him. They came to this Volkswagen that was shot up and lying over in a ditch with two dead German officers lying in this staff car.

He told Fred Dean, the driver, "Pull over there Fred I want to check those guys out and see if they have any papers or maps on them".

When Fred pulled off onto the shoulder of the road they hit a mine. It killed the driver, Fred Dean, the radio operator Sergeant Bailey and it blew Captain Paddock's leg off. I was really sorry to hear about that. I was in the hospital at the time and someone wrote and told me about that. He was a good man. They were all good men and brave soldiers.

Another excellent officer that I served under was our battalion commander, Major Walker. He was also a professional soldier that commanded our battalion. Everybody just thought he was a great guy. Of course, I didn't know him personally, but he was someone everyone admired.

Over in England he was being flown to a staff meeting in a Piper Cub. These little airplanes were attached to our battalion and were used to go up and spot artillery fire with. He was in this Piper Cub with a pilot that was flying him to a staff meeting. They crashed and burned on the moors and both he and the pilot were killed. That was a tragic loss to our battalion.

An older man replaced him; his name was Colonel Watson. He was a typical Battalion Commander, the type you see in the movies. He was very military and very courageous. He had a big black mustache and although he wasn't very big he had a military bearing that demanded respect. He was a good man; we went into combat with him.

One day he was doing what officers are supposed to do, inspire the troops. We were under fire, in a column, a motorized column of tanks, trucks, etc. We were held up with a blown out bridge. We were under fire and some of the fellas had taken shelter in the ditches along side of the road. Colonel Watson came striding down the road with his bodyguard and he said.

"Alright, let's get this column moving now!"

He was just walking along like he was just out for a walk. Bullets and shrapnel were flying all around. Of course that is what Battalion Commanders are supposed to do. They are supposed to get out there and give the troops inspiration. We called it "drawing fire".

Some of my friends in my battery were characters. Really nice guys, but some of them were characters. One was a fella by the name of Dock Jones. That was his name, D O C K, Dock Jones. He was big, tall, raw boned, southerner that came from Alabama. He was a hard case. He had done a year and a day in a penitentiary for something, assault and battery or something. It was pretty bad so they'd sent him away for a year and a day. He was a pretty tough cookie.

He was our loader; he loaded our gun for us most of the time. He was very good at that and he was an expert rifle shot. Every time we went out on a range he shot expert. He was a good friend of mine.

I had another friend from Camden, NJ Orlando D'Alesandro. He was our mechanic for the guns. He was one of the howitzer mechanics; he worked on the guns when they needed repair.

Another friend from Philadelphia, Francis McGinn from Kensington I believe it was. Another fellow was from Woodstown, Lester Flitcraft. In fact he got rotated when the war was still on. He was an older fellow and had enough points to get rotated. He stopped over to see me when I was home on furlough from the hospital.

Another friend was named Franklin Witterstatter from Beaumont, Texas. He was just a little fella and was always smoking a cigar. He drove a jeep; boy he just loved that jeep. He called the jeep "Josephine". He named it after one of his girlfriends.

Another good friend of mine was Andor Todhunter Nogrady. He was a great big, red-faced Irishman from someplace out in Illinois, near Chicago. He was very intelligent; he had gone to two years of college, got sick of going to school and joined the Army. I think his folks were pretty well to do. He never lacked for spending money. He was quite a character and was always getting into trouble. Not serious trouble, just minor stuff. He always had to pull extra duty. He was a lot of fun, always kept you laughing. He got transferred out of the outfit when we were in England. They put him in the Assault Signal Corps. He landed on Omaha Beach with the signal outfit. He never made it to the beach; he got machine-gunned when he was in the water. He lay behind one of the obstacles just about all day. He wound up with not only the wounds, but also pneumonia. I think that was the end of the war for him although he did survive his wounds.

Andor was such a big hearted guy. He was showing me a picture of his dog; he had a Beagle Hound. I was admiring this Beagle hound; I had done a lot of hunting before I went in the Army. I was telling him.

"Boy, I'd sure like to have a Beagle hound to run rabbits with."

He said, "Would ya? Gosh, she's going to have a litter. I'll send you a puppy."

So I thought, "Yeah, he wouldn't do that."

A few months later my mother got a telephone call from the railway office to go over to the railway express and pick up this crate. Sure enough, he'd sent me two puppies! My mother kept them for me until I got out of the Army.

I had them for quite a while, even after Carolyn and I were married. But two dogs were too much for a young married couple to keep so I gave one away. I gave the female, Nellie away and kept the male, Ned. He was a pretty good rabbit hound. He developed heart worm after a few years and I had to have him put to sleep.

That was the kind of a guy Andor was. If you told him,

"Gee I'd like to have that."

He'd say, "Okay I'll get it for you."

He was just like that.

Our time in Fort Dix was pretty uneventful. I managed to get home quite a few times because I was fairly close to home, about 45–50 miles. We just settled down to a summer of training.

10

Finally in the early fall we got our orders that we were going to ship out and go to Florida, Camp Gordon Johnston, Florida for amphibious training. When we heard amphibious training we knew what was ahead for us.

We started preparing our equipment for the move to Florida. Finally we were getting all set to go, ready to leave in two or three days. Somehow or another I came in late off a pass. Captain Paddock called me in to the orderly room.

He said, "I should bust you, but we need a good gunner like you. I'm not supposed to give non-commissioned officers extra duty, but I'm not going to give you extra duty, I'm going to give you a special detail. You're going to work with the kitchen crew on the train on the way to Florida."

This meant I was on KP. But it turned out pretty neat because it was a lot of fun. We had our kitchen set up in a boxcar. I helped the kitchen crew prepare the meals, but most of the time I just sat on the side of the box car with my feet hanging out the door looking at the scenery going by. The train was going really, really slow as we headed down into Florida. We went down through Tallahassee and saw Spanish moss hanging off the trees; I'd never seen anything like that. It was really out in the middle of nowhere.

Finally we got to a place called Carabel, Florida. The town of Carabel is about two miles outside of Camp Gordon Johnston.

It was a very primitive camp. We had barracks, but they didn't have any floors. They had dirt floors. We just had wash houses, very similar to what we had in Fort Sill except that we were in barracks instead of tents. It was a very interesting experience.

I met a fellow that I went to high school with. He was in the training outfit. He was in the amphibious engineers. They were the ones that trained us for the amphibious landings.

Our barracks was right on the beach, right on the Gulf. The Gulf was beautiful, with a beautiful beach of white sand. Carabel is sixty miles due south of Tallahassee, Florida.

In our spare time we could go swimming and fishing but we didn't have a whole lot of spare time.

Everybody had to know how to swim. The ones that didn't know how to swim had to learn. They had to go and take swimming lessons.

They had a tower in the middle of a lake to simulate the side of a ship. We had to be able to jump off this tower with all our equipment on and be able to swim maybe fifty yards (I don't remember how far). It was pretty tough, even for good swimmers. I always considered myself a fair swimmer, but it was tough swimming with all that stuff on.

They taught us how to take your pants off, tie knots in the end of the legs and get them full of air and you can use them for an emergency life preserver. All those little tricks. They taught us if you have to jump off the side of the ship never have the strap buckled on your helmet because it would break your neck when you hit the water.

We practiced climbing up and down the cargo nets, because you might have to climb down into the landing craft from the big ship on a cargo net. A cargo net is just a great big rope net they throw over the side. The fellows clamber down through, you've seen it in the newsreels.

We had to learn how to operate all the different boats. They said it would be the Navy or the Coast Guard running these boats; but if something happens to them somebody has to know how to run the boat.

There were Higgins boats and LCVP's and all these small landing craft. It was a lot of fun then, playing around in the water. We'd go out on these boats, ride around on the Gulf, having a grand time.

I had a ten-day furlough, so I went home. When I came back it was getting into November, around Thanksgiving time. We were having maneuvers, amphibious maneuvers.

It had been raining a bit when I got back into camp, after midnight. I got into the barracks and crawled into my bunk and boy, it seemed like I had just shut my eyes when everybody started yelling.

"Come on! Get up! We're falling out!"

We were leaving on this amphibious maneuver they had scheduled. I had just about two or three hours sleep and was really groggy. We got up and got dressed, threw our gear together and fall out. Boy, it was really miserable out!

They marched us down to the dock. We climbed aboard these LCVP's. Which means, Landing Craft Vehicle Personnel. We loaded our tank on the LCVP, climbed aboard and shoved off. The weather was getting worse all the time.

We pulled out into the Gulf, riding around rendezvousing with the other boats. Man, it was really, really miserable! The wind was blowing hard; in fact it was a hurricane. It came up and caught us unaware. In those days we didn't have the weather warning systems that they have now.

The whole division was out in the Gulf in these little boats. Quite a few of them went down and they lost some of the fellas, they drowned. There we were riding around in the dark in this little LVCP. We came across another one that was just about ready to sink; it was full of water. We pulled up along side and took the men off that were aboard. It was a mortar squad in the infantry. They climbed aboard our boat and just as they did their boat went down. It went down like a stone!

Here we were with a tank plus too many men aboard this LCVP. The water was coming in over the sides. We all had our helmets off, bailing water out of this thing with our helmets. There weren't any other boats around, so if ours' sank there wasn't anyone else to pick us up. Finally we made it back to shore. This was quite a rough time.

That storm cost them quite a few men and a lot of boats and equipment. It was just too much for the little landing craft.

The next day there were so many men missing that the pilot that flew the spotter plane, a little piper cub, flew out over the Gulf looking for survivors. He had a radio with him and he'd radio when he'd spotted a boat or somebody floating in the water. He'd radio back and they'd send boats out to try and pick them up.

I understand he got the Air Medal for flying out to sea so far in one of those little land-based planes. If his motor quit or if he had any trouble there wasn't any way he could put that thing down in the water. Those planes weren't designed to land on water.

All in all it was quite an experience.

Then they started training us on the LCT's, which is a landing craft tank. It's a much larger vessel and has a capacity to hold four tanks, four ammunition trailers and a small jeep or a weasel, which is a jeep with tracks on it.

The LCT's have a ramp on the front; just like a big barge but it does have a cabin in the after-end. They also have a couple of anchors on the stern. When pulling onto the beach they ground themselves on the beach. Just before hitting the beach two anchors are released, called kedge anchors. There are big winches on these anchors and when pulling up to the beach these anchors get dropped a little bit off shore.

Then the crew pays the line out; run up on the beach and drop the ramp in order to unload the tanks and men. Then they use the winch to pull the boat back off of the beach; otherwise it would be stranded. This is called "kedging the boat off the beach".

These were pretty interesting craft to be on because they were a lot bigger than the LCVP's that we were riding around on before. The whole battery could go in on one boat. These were the types of craft we made the landings with in Normandy. These were they smallest vessels to go all the way across the channel and make the landings.

For training, we made a number of amphibious landings in Florida. It seems to me that these landings were always under the cover of darkness. I remember one night we landed on the beach there in Florida; boy it was pitch black, you couldn't see a thing. We made it a practice that the Sergeant and the Corporal would get out and walk to lead the tank to show the driver where to go. It was so dark and there was a great big stump on the beach right where the position was that we had to go into.

The Greek walked on one side of it and I walked on the other, neither one of us saw the stump. Our tank ran right up onto the stump! It was just low enough that the tank ran up on it and it lifted one of the treads up off the ground and it just spun around. We had the darndest time getting the tank off of that stump! We had to get a bunch of rocks to throw under the treads. Finally another tank came along and pulled us off. It was a little embarrassing for us; but really we never saw that stump because it was so dark.

We used to make these landings then be ashore for four or five days firing and practicing. After a couple of months in Camp Gordon Johnston we got orders to move to Fort Jackson, South Carolina.

11

Back on the train we went with all our equipment and moved up to Fort Jackson, South Carolina. We kind of figured we were on our way overseas. Rumors were running around like mad, they always are in the Army. Training intensified even more and they were starting to give us more of an orientation for the European Theater, which we figured, was where we were headed.

We just settled down to more intense training. Finally it got to be around Christmas time. On Christmas Eve I was put on special MP detail in Columbia, S.C. which was the nearest town to Fort Jackson. I had about four or five men under me. We were temporary MP's, this was the only time I was ever an MP.

Our duty was to go into the police station and hang around the police station. The station MPs would bring in the drunks, of course on Christmas Eve a lot of GI's would go out and get "blind drunk". We'd bring in the drunks and then separate the Fourth Division drunks from the other guys. When there was a truckload, we'd take them back to the camp and drop them off at their outfits.

I didn't go back to camp with the truck. I stayed at the police station; it was a civilian police station and an MP station. A couple of guys would ride in with the truck. I forget how many truckloads of drunks we took in. It was quite an experience. Talk about seeing the seamy side of life that was really it. Some of these guys were really stinking!

I remember this one guy, just a little fella, out of the Fourth Division. He came in and boy he was "bombed out of his mind"! These two big MPs brought him in and he was giving them a hard time. They slammed him onto a bench along side of the room and told him to sit there.

Man, he wasn't about to sit there! He wanted to get up and explain to the desk Sergeant that he wasn't really drunk. After a while he jumped up, picked up the bench and threw it half way across the room!

Those two MPs pulled out their billy clubs and worked him over something awful. But he was still hollering, yelling, kicking and screaming so they threw him into a cell. They told him to "shut up" and they'd be back to get him after a while.

He wouldn't shut up, he was hollering and yelling. They had a bunch of homeless people in the jail because they didn't have any place to sleep. It was kind of cold and since it was Christmas time the jail had opened up for the homeless people. Well, this drunk was waking everybody up. By this time it was the wee hours of the morning.

The MPs went into the cell and handcuffed the guy to the bars of the cell and shoved a handkerchief in his mouth and gagged him. He still wasn't content to be quiet and he started kicking the cell door. It made an awful racket.

So the MPs said, "Come over and help us with this guy. Go in there and take off his shoes."

I said, "That guy is going to kick me."

They said, "He won't kick you. If he kicks you it will be the last guy he kicks. He won't kick that cell door much with his bare feet."

So I went in there and I told him: "Look buddy, just let me take your shoes off or these guy are really going to work you over if you don't."

So, he was pretty quiet and I took his shoes off. After a while he must have passed out. I think he was on the last load that we took back to camp that night.

I don't know how many truckloads of guys we took back to camp. The soldiers were really on a tear. It was Christmas Eve and I guess they figured it was the last Christmas Eve that they would see in the United States for a while. For some of them it *was* the last Christmas Eve they ever saw!

There were two kinds of MPs. There were Station MPs and Division MPs. The Station MP's stayed right at the camp and never moved out with the troops. The Division MPs were part of the division and went overseas with us. The station MP's were brutal but the Division MPs took it kind of easy on you if you were from their outfit. The station MPs were a mean bunch. Some of them were really sadistic! I don't know what they ever wound up doing in civilian life. They sure didn't have very good training to be preachers, I'll tell you that!

12

In a very short time we got our orders to move out again. This time it was to Camp Kilmer. That's called the Port of Embarkation. As soon as we heard we were going to Camp Kilmer we knew we were on our way. We packed everything up again, loaded everything on the train and headed to Camp Kilmer.

We were only at Camp Kilmer for a very short time. We just got some shots; our records reviewed to make sure that everybody's record was in order.

I'll never forget over the latrine door, of the barracks I was in, some guy had made a sign. It said, "If you can read this sign you'd better give your soul to God, cause your ass is going overseas!"

From then on there were no more passes. Nobody got off the base; we were all restricted to the area. Time was filled with checking equipment, making sure everybody had all his equipment and it was in good order.

In maybe a week to ten days we got an order to move out. We got on a train in the middle of the night. It is just a short journey from Camp Kilmer to the port of New York.

It was the middle of the night; the train was all blacked out with all the curtains drawn. Nobody was allowed to open a curtain on the train because they didn't want anyone to know it was a troop train with troops that was headed to the port of N.Y. The train pulled into the port, right up to the dock. We got off the train and formed up in formation and as they called your name off you had to holler out and go up the gangway onto the ship.

The ship we were on was the Capetown Castle, it was the sister ship to the Morro Castle, which burned and drifted ashore at Asbury Park back in the 30's. It was a British ship, a fairly nice ship, but it was getting along in years, probably pretty slow. But that didn't matter because we were going over in a convoy and the convoy can only go as fast as the slowest ship in the convoy. I'm sure there were some ships in the convoy that were slower than we were.

We got aboard the ship and they had people standing around directing us where to go. Boy, it seemed like we went down the ladders, down the ladders and down the ladders one deck after another. Finally we came to this big compartment that we were going to be bunking in.

We had bunks from the deck to the overhead, in other words, from the floor to the ceiling. The bunks were only about 18-20 inches apart in height, just enough room to slide in. They were really packing us on board.

I think our whole division went over on two ships. One was the Capetown Castle and I forget the name of the other one. We pulled out the next morning. It was quite a thrill going out of the New York harbor, passing the Statue of Liberty. Looking at it wondering when you were going to see it again, or *IF* you were going to see it again.

We pulled out of the harbor and went on out to sea and forming up with the convoy. I understand it was the biggest convoy up to that time to go across the Atlantic.

This was the first or second week in January. Needless to say it was bitter cold, you couldn't stay up on deck much so we had to stay below in our quarters. Boy, there was no air! Of course there was no such thing as air conditioning, hardly any ventilation. It wasn't too long before the place smelled like a stable! All these guys in there and we only got to take a shower every other day or so. They gave us salt-water soap because we were showering with salt water. It's just like taking a piece of wood and trying to work up lather! I could never get up a lather!

Then there were the chow lines. Seemed like by the time that you got your chow for breakfast it was time to get back in line for lunch! The line was so long; it wound up and down the corridors, passageways and deck. That was quite an experience.

We whiled away the time playing cards, shooting craps and reading. All the things soldiers do to pass time, batting the breeze. Everybody was passing rumors back and forth all the time. Finally, Captain Paddock got us all together and gave us an orientation speech about where we were going. That's when we finally knew we were headed for England.

The Battery Commander gave each of us a little book explaining how different it would be from the United States. The book explained different names for things in England: There wasn't a hood on the car, it was a bonnet; a windshield was a windscreen, gasoline was petrol. They tried to give us a lesson on the currency. How the English pounds, shillings and pence worked; it was all Greek to us!

When we got to England and went into a store to buy anything we would just reach in to our pockets, pull out a handful of coins and hold it out for the storekeeper and say, "Here, take how much it is." We couldn't figure it out, but after awhile we got the hang of it.

My friend Andor Nogrady had been assigned to be a member of the gun crew on the ship. They had some guns on the ship, a three inch gun up on the bow and another on the stern, maybe a four or five inch. They had 20-mm anti-aircraft machine guns on the upper deck. They gave Andor a crash course on firing the 20-millimeter. He was put on duty every six hours for a couple hours at a time.

I used to go up and stand or sit with him to pass the time. It was interesting but he never got a chance to fire the 20-mm because we didn't have any air raids going across.

We did have a couple of sub scares. There were destroyers running around all the time and it was quite a sight seeing this great big convoy. I learned one thing…in order to keep their place in the convoy these ships would drop a large float off the stern on a big long line, 200 or 300 yards long. They would drag this in back of the ship. The ship in back of them might not see the ship in front of them because of the fog, haze or darkness. But, they could see this thing splashing through the water and they would know how far they were from the ship in front.

They didn't have any collisions that I heard of. They had one ship that was torpedoed, but it was way on the other side of the convoy and we didn't know about it until later.

We were a couple of weeks going across because it was pretty slow. As we pulled into Liverpool we got our first glimpse of the damage which the German bombers had done to England. A lot of the warehouses and buildings had been bombed and the rubble was lying all around. The people were out there working away doing their thing, unloading ships. The place was a real beehive of activity with all the ships coming in and being unloaded. The cranes were swinging all the cargo off the ships and onto the docks.

13

After a while we got off the ship and onto another train. We had no idea where we were headed, they didn't tell us. We found out later that we were heading to the southern part of England, to Devonshire. Devonshire was beautiful, open country. Rolling, grassy hills, I guess they raise a lot of cows and sheep down there. It was nice; I enjoyed the time I spent in England. It was a nice country. The people were very pleasant and they treated us well.

We headed for our camp, Denbury Camp. It had originally been a British Army hospital. They had moved out to other quarters and they refurbished and made it into a camp. It was near a town called Newton Abbott in the southern part of England.

The facilities at the camp were not quite large enough to accommodate all of us. For instance, if you wanted to get a shower with hot water you had to get up about three o'clock in the morning. The hot water boiler wasn't large enough. We'd have the guards wake us up at two or three o'clock. We'd get up, take a hot shower and go back to bed. Otherwise you had to take a cold shower and that wasn't much fun.

About a week after we were settled in our camp I started having trouble hearing, in fact I was almost totally deaf. When I went on sick call they sent me to the hospital and after an examination the doctor told me that they were going to send me back to the States. Well, I was very upset to say the least. I hadn't come all this way to go back home while my outfit went into action. When I got back to the Battery I went down to the Orderly Room and asked to see Captain Paddock. I explained my problem and told him the doctors wanted to send me back and couldn't he please put me in another position where my hearing wouldn't matter. I knew that I couldn't continue to be a gunner as we had to listen for the fire commands but perhaps I could be a machine-gunner or an ammunition handler.

Captain Paddock asked me "Can you make out alright on the telephone"?

I replied, "Yes Sir, I can hold it up against the side of my head and hear O.K."

He said, "I'll send you over to the Fire Direction Center and see how it works out."

The Fire Direction Center was located in a large tent some distance from our camp and was the direct link between all 5 Batteries in the Battalion. It was the place where the fire of the 3 firing Batteries was coordinated in case there was a target of such size that the Battalion Commander decided all 12 guns of the Battalion would fire on it at once. My job was to man a telephone that was linked to Battery "B" and to record all the changes of deflection so that at any time our Battery could be brought to bear on the Battalion target. There was a man from each Battery in the Battalion all talking to their respective Batteries. It was a hectic but interesting job but I was only there for about a week as my hearing gradually returned.

When I felt that I could handle my old job as a gunner I went back to the doctor. After he examined me he said that it must have been the change of climate that affected my ears and that I would probably be all right now. When I reported to Captain Paddock he transferred me back to my old job in the 4th gun section. It was a disturbing episode, but it turned out OK.

Our training continued and our maneuvers were up on the Moors. We'd go to a place called Exmoor. The moors are a strange part of the country. They are up on a plateau. You had to go uphill; I remember, get up the top of a good size hill and there was a plateau. It was very marshy. You could stand on the ground and jump up and down and you could see the ground undulate about a hundred yards away. It was quite an odd place. We practiced our maneuvers up there. There was a firing range up there to fire our 105's.

So we settled down into more training, but this was pretty serious training because we knew we were heading into combat soon.

There was a place called Slapton Sands down on the channel coast. It was a seashore resort. The military had cleared all the civilians out; they just commandeered the whole town. They went in there and told the people to get out.

We used to practice our landings at this place called Slapton Sands. The terrain was very similar to the terrain in Normandy where we were scheduled to land. There was a beach with sand dunes and a little town. In back of the town was a marshy area.

We pulled two or three landings there. We'd go out in the channel and ride around on the landing craft and then land. Sometimes we'd use live ammunition to practice firing. We would practice firing off the boats with these 105's. That was a tricky maneuver to hit anything firing off a small craft. You had to time the waves; sometimes you couldn't hold the gun sight on anything. You had to wait until the target came into view and then fire. It was a challenge.

One time we had a big maneuver scheduled, it was called "Operation Tiger". It was going to be our whole division practicing this landing at Slapton Sands.

We had a lot of attached outfits too. There were Navy outfits, engineer outfits and signal corps. They were all involved in this simulated landing.

One night we were out in the channel. There was a couple of Canadian or British destroyers supposed to be guarding the convoy. But, they weren't on the same radio frequency and there was a mix up in orders. One of the destroyers had to head to port and the other was unaware.

In the middle of the night a couple of German E boats managed to get into the convoy and torpedoed two or three LST's. It was pandemonium! The destroyer that was left guarding us didn't engage the PT boats at all.

Fortunately our boat was on the other side of the convoy. We heard this racket and saw the glow in the sky and saw the fire. We couldn't figure what in the world was going on.

Then we heard these two engines, sounded like a couple airplanes coming, only they were right down on sea level. Then these two German E boats came flying past us, they were really moving. Of course everything was blacked out and we didn't even know what they were. Everybody was saying, "Wow, what was that?" We found out later that it was two German E boats. We lost about 800 men in that operation. They say there were bodies washing ashore for a week later onto the beach.

The next day they got us all together by outfit. An order came down from Headquarters telling us not to say anything to ANYONE about this operation. They didn't want the Germans to find out that we had such a strong showing of force in one place because the Germans might be able to figure out that the landings were imminent.

Under the threat of court martial we were told not to discuss this with anybody. In fact, they buried all the bodies in a big scooped out common grave near the beach.

The families were never even notified until later. The families were notified after D-Day as though they had been casualties of D-Day, but this had been about a month before.

It was quite a mess. The commanders were so afraid of an information leak. Among those missing there were ten officers that had the knowledge of where and when we were going to land in Normandy.

The big brass was in a big sweat to recover these bodies and make sure that these officers hadn't fallen into enemy hands and divulged this information. I understand they recovered nine of the bodies, but they never recovered the tenth one. They were worried about this. But obviously he was just lost; the landing was a surprise for the Germans.

This whole thing remained a secret until sometime in the 1960's. An English woman thought about what she had seen when she was a little girl. She had seen all these trucks going by with bodies in them and the bodies on the beach. She had never heard any explanation and wondered, as an adult, what in the world had happened.

She talked to some newspaper and they started an investigation and finally came up with what had happened at Slapton Sands. It was called "The Mystery of Slapton Sands". There was a television documentary about it and the story was in all the papers. I understand that now there is a memorial on the beach right there for the men that died in this exercise.

It was strange that nobody had said anything about it for all those years. Of course we had been told not to. The news never got out; it was a strange thing.

14

One day our whole division was scheduled to be reviewed by General Eisenhower and General Montgomery. Usually, when you pass in review it is on the parade grounds with the divisions band playing and everyone in formation parading past the reviewing stand. However this was to be different. The whole division (15,000 men) were dressed in combat gear, on foot, with rifles slung, walking in single file on each side of the road.

General Eisenhower and General Montgomery came walking down the road in the opposite direction. It must have been quite an impressive sight for them, but for us it was just another long, dusty walk. But it gave us an opportunity to get a closer look at the men who would order us into battle. Little did we know that we were also looking at a future President of the United States.

Later that day General Montgomery pulled into our battery bivouac area in a jeep. Captain Paddock lined us all up in formation. General Montgomery climbed up on the hood of the jeep and called out

"Gather round!"

So, we broke ranks and gathered around the jeep. The General proceeded to give us a rousing speech in his clipped British accent. It was quite a pep talk and I still remember his closing line:

"Go over there and kill those bastards!"

After his speech he spoke to a few of us individually and shook hands. He wanted to know where we were from, how long we had been in the Army etc.

It was a good experience to meet a famous fighting General. I understand that General Eisenhower visited some of the other outfits. I really would have liked to meet him.

All of us in the 4th Infantry Division were very proud to be part of such a famous outfit. The 4th had fought with honors in World War I and was one of the best-trained Divisions to be sent into combat in World War II. We were the first sea-born troops ashore in the Normandy Landing and the Division fought with distinction in all the major battles after the Landings.

The 4th Infantry Division suffered 34,309 casualties, nearly 229% of our original 15,000 men Division. These casualties were between June 6, 1944; the D-Day Invasion and May 8, 1945; the end of the war in Europe.[1]

Around the first part of May we started preparing all our equipment for a real serious landing. We had to waterproof our tanks and smear this sticky stuff on every rivet. It took us a couple days to get the tank waterproofed.

All the vehicles had to be waterproofed. The jeeps had these snorkels on their air intake and on their exhaust. The engines were all smeared with stuff to keep the water out. All the big trucks and our tanks would then able to go through about 6 to 8 feet of water. The vehicles were being prepared in case the landing craft didn't get all the way into the beach so they would operate through deep water if necessary. The latter part of May we got our orders to pack everything up and get ready to move out to our marshalling area. The marshalling area was the concentration point were all the troops would concentrate just before going down and loading onto the landing craft.

I can remember we were pulling out of our battery area I guess about 3 o'clock in the morning. It was pitch black. We were all sitting around on the tanks waiting for the order to crank up and move out. It was a misty, typical British early morning. They brought the Red Cross donut wagon in. All the guys were standing around the donut wagon drinking coffee and eating donuts. They had the Red Cross volunteers there giving out our donuts. It was a scene reminiscent of pictures that we'd see from the First World War, all the soldiers standing around with their helmets and their rifles on their shoulders and the Red Cross girls handing out donuts. It was something that sticks in your memory.

We pulled out in a motor convoy down to the marshalling area. There were fences all around this place. Once you got in you just didn't get out. No more passes, no more furloughs, no more anything. You just stayed right there. They had MPs patrolling all around the fences, just like we were in prison. We were living in tents during this time.

I think we were only there about a week. We were having indoctrination about where we were going to land. The commanders had the sand tables set up with little miniatures of the beach and the marshy area. They were pointing out all our objectives; this was really serious business.

We finally got the order to move out, to move onto the landing craft. All climbed aboard the tanks with all our equipment and everything that was going

---

1.   The Division Artillery, 4th Infantry Division, Army & Navy Publishing Company, 234 Main Street, Baton Rouge, LA, 1946.

to go with us. We pulled down to what they called "the hards" which is what we'd call a ramp. This was in Dartmouth.

We had the LCT's; LST's and LSI's all pulled into this place. We loaded onto an LCT. When you load on these things you have to back the tanks on, because you don't turn the tank around when you hit the beach. You want to be ready to pull right straight off, so we had to back it on.

We pulled an ammunition trailer called a caisson. It was an armored trailer full of our 105 ammunition. We had an excellent driver named Potter. He could back the tank around on a dime. We were the last gun off the boat, so we were the first one on. There wasn't enough room for us to have our ammunition trailer hooked up. When we got aboard the ship we had to unhook the caisson and swing it around broadside so it didn't take up as much room and then back the tank up against it. That was fine, but it meant that when we hit the beach we had to wait for the other tanks to get off, pull our tank forward and then jump down and grab the trailer and manhandle it into position. This thing weighed tons and we had to hook it back up before we could get off the boat.

The only time I ever saw a cameraman when we were in combat was when we were loading onto this LCT. There was a cameraman taking film of us backing our tank onto the LCT. I've always looked whenever I saw a newsreel of equipment being loaded on landing craft. I always kept looking to see if I see that shot but I've never seen it yet; so I guess it hit the cutting room floor.

All the practice-training exercises really paid off because the final loading went very smoothly with all the units I saw. We could watch all the ships being loaded because the ships were tied up right alongside of one another along this big wharf. After we got aboard and got everything stowed away we could stand up on top of the tank and watch the other units come in and get loaded on.

Everything went smoothly. There was nobody running around yelling or any confusion. Everybody knew just what to do and they all did their job, really professional.

15

Finally we got ready to cast off for Normandy. The date was June 5, 1944. We ran down this little river in Dartmouth and finally out to sea, to the English Channel. When we got out into the Channel it was awfully rough. The wind was blowing hard, sea was running high and it was raining. Conditions were really bad and some of the fellas were getting seasick.

The LCTs were the smallest craft to go all the way across from one side of the channel to the other. The LCIs and LSTs were larger ships. The small landing craft all got loaded just off the beach of Normandy and made the short run in. But we had to ride our landing craft all the way across and it was one rough ride!

After we got beat around for quite a while, the order came down for us to turn back. Now remember this was June the 5th, the day that the landing was supposed to take place. But because of the severe weather it was postponed.

So we turned back and headed on back to Torquay, which has a big harbor. In fact it is a big seashore resort on the channel coast. We pulled in the harbor in Torquay and dropped anchor and we had no sooner dropped anchor (it seemed to me) then the air raid sirens went off and we had an air raid. But they didn't hit us; they didn't even come close. They were bombing around the city somewhere.

In a little while we pulled the anchor back up and took off again. This time it was the real thing, we kept going. Going across the Channel it was still pretty rough; the storm had died down some but it hadn't quit all together. It was in that little window of opportunity that General Eisenhower decided that we would go. It's a good thing he did because there was no way they could have kept the fellas on those ships until the next tide was right. That would have been another six weeks or so.

We kept going across the channel, I can remember it was about midnight, or a little after, maybe one or two o'clock in the morning. It was pitch black and we were bucking into the waves and we heard all these airplanes coming. They went right over our heads, in fact they went so low we could look up and see them. It was our paratroopers going over to make their jump. They were in C 47's and they all had the white stripes, they called them the "D Day stripes. These stripes were painted on all the allied planes. So if you saw an airplane with white stripes on the wings, you knew it was a friendly plane.

Of course we had air superiority, which was a very fortunate thing. I doubt the landing would have been successful unless we had that air superiority. It was quite a thrill to see those troopers going over because we knew what was ahead of them; or we *thought* we knew.

A couple of hours before we heard the planes go over the Battery Commander came around and handed each of us a mimeographed sheet of paper. It was General Eisenhower's message to the troops and it was quite an inspirational message. It was the one that said,

"You're members of a great crusade and everybody's counting on you. We know your up against great odds but everybody is sure you'll win through to the end."

It was quite an inspiration and as I read that I thought to myself, "Gee, I ought to keep this because this really is a historical document."

In the excitement of the next few days I never knew what happened to it. I wish I had put it in a safe place, but I don't think there were too many safe places at that time.

We proceeded on and just before it broke daylight we started to hear the thunder of the guns. When you hear artillery off in the distance it sounds just like a big thunderstorm. It was the naval guns opening up with the Naval bombardment of the beach.

As we got closer and closer you could pick out the individual gun blasts as they went off.

We were making our final run into the beach. By that time it was daylight. It was about 7:00 in the morning. I think the first wave had hit about 6:30 AM. We passed right off the bow of a battleship. It had all its guns leveled down horizontally; it was lying broadside to the beach. The guns were firing right straight into the beach.

Just as we went past the bow I was looking at this ship and was amazed at how big it was and how small a vessel we were on. As they fired broadside with all the guns the battleship jumped sideways in the water about, I guess ten or twelve feet. It was amazing to see a huge vessel like that being shoved that far sideways in the water with the recoil of those guns.

After we had gotten inland a little ways we saw the havoc those naval guns had made. Boy, they blew holes in the ground that you could put a house in! It was unbelievable. Of course some of those holes could have been bomb craters too. They were really doing a lot of damage.

✗

✗ SEE Fold-out SHEET ON THE bACK COVER.

I don't know how much damage those Naval guns did to the Germans, but they sure did blow down a lot of houses, tore up a lot of orchards and killed a lot of cows.

Just about this time was when we came under fire, our baptism of fire. The shells started coming in and landing all around the boat. The shells were landing around all of the boats and hitting some them, of course.

There was one German gun in particular that seemed to be firing directly at us, because he kept dropping a round right in front of our landing craft. We kept going, didn't take evasive action or anything, just plodded right straight in. He kept firing and they kept falling short and falling short.

We thought, "Oh man, that next one is going to be right in here!" But it never was, he finally stopped firing. Whether he shifted his target to something else or he got knocked out or not, I don't know.

When we were about 1 1/2 miles from the beach our ship approached an LCT that had struck a mine and was sinking. We passed close enough to the vessel so that we could look down into the cargo compartment. I couldn't see anyone alive, but we couldn't have stopped to help them anyway. I learned later that it was a battery of artillery just like ours. It was Battery B of the 29th Field Artillery Battalion. The ship sank with the loss of 59 officers and men.

When we got closer to the beach we came under small arms fire. You could hear the machine guns open up, rattling on the ramp, the steel door at the bow of the ship. The whole bow goes down and that's what you run off on, the ramp of the boat.

We could hear this German machine gunner, boy he was really peppering away at the bow of the ship. We thought, "Man when we pull into the beach and drop that ramp down he's going to be able to shoot right in here." But he never did either. He probably got knocked out before we ever hit the sand.

So, we kept peeking over the side. You'd raise your head up and take a quick peek at the beach to see how close we were coming and it was getting pretty close. Finally we felt the lurch that meant the ship has grounded itself. They had dropped the kedge anchors back just before we grounded. When we heard those kedge anchors go down we knew we were really close. Then we felt the lurch and came to a sudden stop.

It was really a thrill to hear that ramp go down. A ramp makes a lot of noise, all those chains and everything when the ramp is dropped. It was thrilling to hear that ramp go down because you know you are on foreign soil and somebody was doing his best to shoot you.

We had our tanks all started and warmed up ready to take off. We did that on our final run in. Our tanks were just idling. The first three guns pulled off and didn't have too much of a problem. We had to pull our gun ahead a little bit, get the armored trailer, swing it around and hook it up.

Well, boy we didn't waste any time doing that! We were working like a bunch of demons to get that thing hooked up. The thing weighed a ton I guess. We got our trailer hooked up and jumped back on the tank; all except the Greek. It was standard operating procedure that the Chief of Section had to lead the tanks off on foot. The reason for that being, if there was a shell hole right there or some kind of an underwater obstacle that nobody had seen before he would see it and be able to direct the tank around it.

I was directing the driver, sitting on the gunner's seat looking over the shield, following the Greek off. He got down into the water, which was about up to his armpits, across his chest. He was plodding through the water and a German opened up on him with a machine gun. This machine gun was kicking up the water all around him. I was looking almost right straight down at him from my perch up on the tank and thought, "Holy mackerel, their just bound to hit him!"

He just kept plodding along; he never even ducked down in the water. I think if it had been me I'd have ducked down into the water, but he just kept plodding along. Finally they stopped firing. Of course in a situation like that you never know what happened.

The Greek walked on up the beach and we followed him. Then he clambered aboard our tank. When we got up on the beach our orders were to go right up to the sea wall. Where we landed there was a sea wall, about a five-foot concrete sea wall. It was all pockmarked with shells and bullet holes in it.

On the way up, I looked around. It was quite a sight. There were all kinds of vehicles and some were burning. Some tanks with their tracks blown off and some vessels that had grounded and couldn't get back off the beach. They had hit the beach so hard they couldn't back off and the Germans were shooting them full of holes. It was really a chaotic scene. There were quite a few GI's lying around on the beach, some were wounded, some were dead.

We pulled up to the sea wall, shut the engine off and prepared for action. It didn't take us too long because we were really professionals at that. The next thing was to get out and dig our personal hole. If you weren't actually on the gun firing you could get down in the hole and take cover. So we got off, dug our holes and were all set to go.

It seems that there was a barrage balloon crew on every landing vessel that came across the channel. This was a crew of about four or five fellas that had a winch, a big heavy winch that was hand operated. However, it was small enough that four men could carry it. They had this barrage balloon that they towed on a long steel cable, to prevent the enemy airplanes from coming in and strafing (machine gunning the troops). It kept the enemy aircraft up at a height above the barrage balloons. If the Germans came down and tried to strafe they'd hit that cable with their wing it would slice the wing right off the plane.

When the vessels hit the beach, these fellas would grab the winch and bring the winch in and set up on the beach. So, all along the beach the barrage balloons were protecting us.

I can remember we came under some mortar fire. I was lying down in my hole looking up in the sky, watching a barrage balloon. All of a sudden there was a loud crack close by and the barrage balloon started going straight up in the air. A shell had hit right at the base of the winch and cut the cable. The barrage balloon was loose and I think it wiped out the crew of that barrage balloon. The balloon took off, going somewhere into the stratosphere.

Our forward observer was a First Lieutenant, Lt. Caldwell. He had gone in with Infantry with the first wave. He had gone inland far enough and found a tree. Of course there weren't any trees on the beach, just off the beach were sand dunes and then over the sand dunes was a marshy area. There were only a couple of roads, causeways, across the marshy area. We had to wait until the Infantry had secured the roads before we could get off the beach and get across the marsh. There was no way we could get across the marsh; all the tanks would have gotten bogged down. We had to wait until the causeways were cleared.

Lt. Caldwell had gone inland with the infantry and climbed a tree to get observation. While he was up in the tree an Infantryman came along, saw him up in the tree, thought he was a sniper and started shooting at him with his rifle!

He came down out of the tree hollering, "Don't shoot, don't shoot!"

He was almost down, the guy kept missing him, and he had one foot up in the air and the guy shot him right through the bottom of the foot. So our forward observer had to go back to the hospital and somebody else took his place.

As it turned out we never got a chance to fire even one round off the beach because we didn't have any observation. It was just one of those circumstances of war.

Dock Jones and I crawled up on top of the sand dune and we were looking out over top of the sand dune to see how the battle was going to take this marshy area. It was quite a sight. The marshy areas was in front of us and down a little bit lower than we were, so we had ring side seats to this battle. The Infantrymen were slogging through the marsh and every once in a while you'd see a fella open up with a flame-thrower on a pillbox. We couldn't even see the pillboxes; they were so well camouflaged. We couldn't see them from where we were, but we could hear the machine guns, the rifles, hand grenades and mortars going off. It was quite a battle.

While we were observing we saw the causeway off to our left a little bit and it went straight across the marsh and made a hard curve off to the right. This was the causeway we were going to have to go down after the marsh was cleared.

There was a farmhouse where the road curved, facing down the causeway. There were a couple of tanks that had started down the causeway, one in back of the other. They couldn't go two abreast, as it was too narrow. We saw them churning down the causeway firing with their turret guns and machine guns. All at once the whole front of the farmhouse flopped down! It was a camouflaged gun position, hiding a German 88-gun crew! They opened up on those two tanks. With the first shot they hit the first tank, it wheeled around and fell over into the ditch. With the second round they got the second tank, it started to burn and also went off into the ditch.

Later on that afternoon when we were going down the causeway ourselves we passed those two knocked out tanks. The first one, the 88 had gone right in the front end and out the back. The second one had caught fire and burned up. It was quite an impressive, and at the same time, discouraging sight to see how easily our tanks could be knocked out with the 88's. This was a very powerful weapon that the Germans had. At that time we didn't have anything that could stand up against them.

Late in the afternoon we got off the beach, got inland and pulled into a firing position. By that time it was almost nightfall as we got the guns prepared for action. We had another forward observer. He radioed back the coordinates to us and we commenced firing on these targets.

After it got really dark the firing slacked off a while and a few of us were able to get down and dig our holes. That's what you do at nighttime; you have to sleep in a hole because you never know when a shell is going to come in. If you are sleeping on the ground, above ground, the chances of getting hit are a lot higher than if you are down in a slit trench or a foxhole. It is tough sleeping in a foxhole so most of us dug slit trenches where we could stretch out.

16

I had discovered when we were on maneuvers that your steel helmet makes a pretty comfortable pillow. You just put the steel helmet on your head lay on your back and the harness of the steel helmet kind of acts like a pillow. Keeps your head up off the ground and you still have some protection.

The steel helmet was quite a good piece of equipment. It came in two pieces; the helmet liner had a harness inside that fit around your head and was adjustable for different size heads. The steel helmet fit over the liner, which had a chinstrap on it. You could take the steel part off and use it as a pot or a bucket. You could cook in it, bail the boats out with it, and carry water in it. It was a very useful piece of equipment and it always felt good to have it on your head in combat because you never knew when it might just save your life.

I've heard a couple of tales about fellas that got hit in the helmet. One fella I knew personally was lying out in the middle of the road. He was in the wire section. They came under machine gun fire and he dropped down and was lying prone in the middle of the road. A bullet hit right at his forehead, but it hit between the steel helmet and the helmet liner. It just followed the helmet around and dropped off on the back of his neck.

He brought the helmet back to show us. It had a furrow along the top of it, like a crease along the top of it where this bullet had creased it. That was really a close call for him and he was awfully glad he had that steel helmet on.

The first few days and nights after we landed were very, very hectic. We were firing most of the time. When we weren't firing, we were moving to another position. None of us got much rest at all. We didn't have a whole lot to eat except for rations. But when you're under so much stress you don't have much of an appetite.

When we were on the landing craft, which was run by a Coast Guard crew. They were real veterans. They'd been in invasions of Sicily, Italy, Salerno and Anzio. They had hit some hot beachheads and knew what they were doing.

The crew had piled up a pile of these ten-in-one rations on the deck. These rations came in a cardboard box. There were enough rations in a box to feed ten men for one day or one man for ten days or two men for five days or whatever.

There was a whole pile of these rations stacked up right along side of our ammunition trailer. We looked at that and thought, "Boy, chow's not going to be easy to get around here. Why don't we just help ourselves to some of these rations."

They were going to unload them onto the beach after the ship hit the beach anyway.

Under the cover of darkness we got as many of those boxes that we could fit in odd places on our tank. There wasn't a whole lot of room, but we found room enough for some of those ten-in-one rations.

So for the first week or so, we ate fairly well. But for the first couple days nobody had much of an appetite because we were busy firing and moving to new positions.

On about the second or third day I had an awful pain in my side. It was way down low and was really hurting. I thought, "Oh my gosh, I must have appendicitis."

That was the first thing that entered my mind, that my appendix was giving me trouble. It hurt so badly I could hardly straighten up. I asked one of the fellas to help me down to the battalion aid station to get me something for it.

We walked on down the road, Joe Viruso and I. He was helping me down; he was my assistant gunner. We walked down to the aid station that was set up in an orchard under a tarp. There were a lot of orchards around there. They had dug a big hole and our battalion doctor was down in this hole.

I had to wait in line as there were a few wounded guys also waiting there. There weren't too many, not many guys had been hit at that time. Finally it came my turn to go in and see the doctor.

He said, "What's the matter?"

I said, "Boy, I have an awful pain in my side. I think I might have appendicitis."

He checked me over and said, "When was the last time you had a good sleep?"

I said, "Jeez, I don't know. I guess it was in the marshalling area. We didn't sleep much on the boat and I haven't slept much since we've been in Normandy the last couple days."

Then he said, "When was the last hot meal you had?"

I said, "Well, I guess that was in the marshalling area too."

He said, "Here, I'll give you this pill and this can of soup. This is a can of self-heating soup."

I had never seen anything like this before. The can that he gave me, I think was tomato soup. The can looked like a big firecracker because it had a big fuse coming out the top. It was self-heating. You would light the fuse and it would burn down the powder train down through the middle of the can and the soup was in like a cylinder around this center part of the can. After the thing burnt out, then you open up the top and pour the soup out and it was hot! It really worked. Boy it was delicious! I took the pill, ate the soup, I lay down, passed out and slept six or seven hours straight through. When I woke up I felt fine. That was the end of my appendicitis.

17

While I'm telling about the medical profession I will tell you a little bit about our medics. Each company in the Infantry and each battery in the Artillery had a medical corpsman that was a member of the outfit but he didn't carry a weapon. He patched you up when you got hurt or wounded. We made fun of them because they didn't fight and they didn't carry a weapon. They weren't supposed to under the Geneva Convention rules. I understand they did in the Pacific, but they didn't in Europe.

We sometimes spoke disparagingly about them and to them. We called them "pill rollers" and a couple other choice names, all in good fun. The one we had was a real nice guy. But I'll tell you that when you get in combat and you get hurt or get hit they sure look good. They help you out and bandage you up and get you ready for the Battalion aid station. They'd be the first line of medical assistance that anybody would see when they got hit. I have to really take my hat off to them. A lot of them did heroic acts, going out and taking care of fellas that had been hit. They would go out in the open and drag them in, or bandage them up under fire. I can't speak too highly of the medics. Even though everyone made fun of them in training, no one made fun of them when we were in combat.

Each Battalion had a Battalion doctor that was a certified doctor. They had been physicians in civilian life. The doctors were all officers; the medics were enlisted men. Our Battalion doctor was named Doc Willey. He was a Major, but everybody just called him Doc. He wasn't much on military courtesy. I guess he knew his business, we never had any complaints.

He used to give us lectures during training on sanitation, venereal diseases, hygiene and things like that. I can remember one time Captain Paddock got the Battery together and we were sitting around the barracks outside in the shade. Doc Willey was speaking to us.

He said, "Look fellas, you know that sooner or later we are going to go into combat and a lot of you are pretty apprehensive about getting wounded. You've all been hurt sometime in your life. Everyone has broken a leg, been burned or scraped. Just remember even though you might get wounded, you won't feel any more pain than you have already felt at sometime in your life. The human body has a way of dealing with pain. If you have too much pain you pass out or go into shock. Don't worry about the pain, you've all felt as much pain as you are ever going to feel."

I don't know how true it was, but it worked out that way with me.

18

I spoke about seeing the C 47's going over the morning of D-Day with all of the paratroopers getting ready for their jump. The paratrooper's mission was to drop inland. The101st Airborne and the 82nd Airborne were the two divisions that dropped in our area.

One of them had to secure the town of St. Mere Eglise. This was the nearest good-sized town to the beach where we hit. They were supposed to work their way back toward us as we came in from the sea. We would relieve them after that.

Once the paratroopers accomplished their mission they went back to England and prepared for the next operation requiring paratroops. Some of the other missions were to secure the floodgates at the marshy area.

It seems that the Germans had large floodgates that held back big water impoundments. If there was a landing they were prepared to open the floodgates and flood the whole marshy area. So instead of being marsh it would be a large river. That was another mission that the paratroopers had to accomplish. They must have done that because the Germans never had a chance to flood the area where I was.

Everyone has seen in the movies how a paratrooper got his parachute caught on a steeple in St. Mere Eglise. We went through that town two or three days after D-Day. Parachutes were hanging all over the place and I saw the one that was hanging off the church steeple, but I didn't know the story behind it. The fella had been taken down by that time of course.

The paratroopers had a dangerous, tough job. When they landed they were scattered all over the place. None of them dropped into the drop zone where they were supposed to be or very few of them did. Most of them were off by themselves and it was almost like Indian fighting, guerilla warfare. They were sneaking around and finally they would meet up with another trooper and then a couple more and they would form their units that way. I knew a lot of paratroopers from being in the hospital and became good friends with them. They had some really good stories to tell. I'll tell you a few of them later.

The troopers had to work their way back toward us. Purple was the color that identified friendly troops. The paratroopers all had these little rolls of purple streamers in their pockets. When they started to get near the Allied troops or the

American forces they would tie these purple things around their helmets or their arms.

I saw a group of paratroopers coming back through the lines. They had captured a German motorcycle; it was an odd motorcycle. It was a troop carrier. It had motorcycle handlebars and front wheel, but on the back it had tracks instead of a wheel. It was like a little tank and on each side of these tank treads was a couple of benches. It would carry about three men on each bench. So you could carry six or seven guys on this motorcycle.

These guys came back on this motorcycle with purple streamers tied to the handlebars so we knew they were friendly troops. They were a happy bunch when they came back through the line and were safe again with us.

I saw another paratrooper that came back riding a horse with a purple streamer tied to the horse's tail. He had captured the horse. The Germans used a lot of horses. They had horse-drawn artillery and supply wagons. We had motor vehicles, but they relied very heavily on horses. Their horses suffered tremendously because they couldn't take cover under shellfire. There were dead horses and cows lying all over the place.

Normandy was an apple orchard and dairy country. There were a lot of cows lying in the fields. A dead cow looks very strange because she fills up with gas and her legs stick straight out.

These paratroopers did a real fine job and they fought very hard for two or three days, some of them longer than that. When they finally accomplished their mission, or were relieved, they would go back to reform, get re-equipped and wait for the next parachute drop.

A different type of airborne troop was the glider troops. They were still airborne but instead of jumping out of the airplanes they flew in gliders and had to land the glider before the soldiers aboard could get out. The glider troops were not volunteers, some of them could have volunteered for it, but most of them had just been ordered into the glider outfit.

Paratroopers were all volunteers because it was a dangerous assignment and the Army just wanted the "cream of the crop". They wanted fellas who were willing to volunteer for these risky missions.

The glider pilots and glider troops all did a great job too. The pilots that piloted the gliders were mostly officers. The gliders didn't have an engine. Once they cut loose from the C 47 tow planes there was only one way to go, and that was down. Gliders could glide around for a little bit, but they had to look quickly for a place to land.

Landing a glider can be tricky. Most of the landings were actually controlled crashes and some of them weren't that controlled. They kept bringing in reinforcements on the second day, known to us as D plus 1. These reinforcements came in by gliders for several days after the invasion, but we had moved out of the area.

I remember one time we were set up in a gun position in the hedgerow country. There was an open field along side of us. A couple of these gliders were trying to get into the field. One of them came down right alongside of our tank and made a pretty good landing. The other one came in and he got too close to the hedgerow. Gliders don't have any brakes on them; they stop by the friction of running along the ground. The pilot didn't have enough room and ran right into this hedgerow and the glider stopped. The gliders had a 37-mm anti-tank gun inside. The force of the landing caused it to come right out the front of the glider with fellas hanging all over it. This impact killed or wounded the men making an awful mess.

The glider troops deserve a lot of credit because what they did was a tough job. They didn't get reassigned once they landed. The glider troops were there to stay, unlike the paratroopers that went back. The Army tried to get the glider pilots back and get them ready for the next drop. But the troops themselves just became part of the Infantry outfits where they had landed.

A lot of gliders were flown in to Normandy. When I was being evacuated back to England by plane, we took off from a fighter strip and circled around over the battlefield to get a little altitude and then head off across the channel. I could look down and see gliders, lying all over the place. Some of them upside down, some with their nose stuck in a hedgerow, others with their wings chopped off. The Germans had planted a lot of poles in the open fields. They called them "Rommel's Asparagus". The Germans had wire strung from the tops of these poles and this made it very, very difficult for the gliders to get through the wire and find a clear place to land.

I understand they got a little extra pay, but they earned every penny of it believe me.

19

I could never get over the awful waste in a war zone. On the beach was where I first noticed it. We had life preservers that were issued to us when we first got on the ship. The life preservers were a rubberized fabric wide belt. You put them around your waist. They had a couple carbon dioxide cylinders in them and if you needed to inflate it there was a certain spot on the belt that you'd squeeze and it would puncture these two little carbon dioxide bottles. They would blow up and support you. There weren't too many fellas that had to use them, we didn't use ours. When you got on dry land you didn't need them anymore. The first thing you would do was squeeze it and inflate the thing, I never saw any that weren't inflated. Then you would throw it away on the beach. There were thousands of them on the beaches.

The roads weren't very improved in that part of Normandy, there were ditches on each side. In those ditches you could see anything and everything you could possibly think of that had been discarded.

The first day we saw a lot of the life preservers in the ditches. But, we also saw gas masks, packs and blankets. I found a Tommy gun in the ditch and confiscated that. It became my Tommy gun. We had a rack inside of the tank made just for a Tommy gun and I put that gun in the rack but I never had a chance to fire it.

When I left the outfit as far as I know it was still inside the tank on that little clip.

One of the fellas found a sniper's rifle. It was a Springfield rifle with a telescopic sight. The Springfields were supposed to be more accurate than the M-1 Garands. This was a bolt action, a real nice rifle. How much he used it I'll never know.

You could find most anything you could think of in the ditches. It never seemed to cease; everywhere we went there was so much debris and waste alongside of the road.

In the course of our travels through Normandy we would go through villages and all the people would be lined up along the side of the road. The villagers would throw flowers at us they were so happy and grateful to be liberated from the Germans. They made apple brandy; they called it Calvodos. They would hand us that brandy and wine. We had plenty of liquid nourishment!

Dock Jones was my #2 man, he would load the gun for me. He kept leaning over the side of the tank, grabbing these bottles of Calvodos and wine from the villagers.

I said, "You know Dock, one of these days somebody's going to hold up one of those German potato mashers grenades and you're going to grab that and blow us all up!"

He said, "Oh no, I wouldn't bring that in here."

The people in Normandy were very happy. It was a pretty rural area and we didn't get through too many towns. I just remember St. Mere Eglise and another town named Montebourg. We had a bad battle there. The Infantry had taken the town, then got pushed back out of the town and had to retake it. We were firing hot and heavy in that battle. There was another well-defended town named Valognes. Our division lost a lot of men taking Valognes. These were the only three towns I think we had been through.

We were heading for Cherbourg, which was the Division's objective. The ordinary soldier doesn't know much about what's going on. The only thing you really know about is your little area that you can look around and see. That's about all you care about too. You don't care about all the tactics and maneuvers, that's for the Generals to worry about.

Your worry is the guy on the other side of the hedgerow that might be dropping a round into a mortar and shooting for you, or drawing a bead on you with a sniper rifle, or machine gun. That's what concerns the ordinary soldier, along with when his next hot meal is going to get there, when's the next time he can change his socks and those sort of things.

The ordinary soldier didn't know a whole lot about where we were or where we were heading. Those in command just informed us that we were landing on Utah Beach in Normandy, which is a peninsula. At the end of this peninsula is the city of Cherbourg which is a harbor port. Our objective was to go right straight across the peninsula and cut off the troops that were occupying Cherbourg and that immediate vicinity. Then we were to make a right turn and advance toward Cherbourg and take the city, which we did. Then Cherbourg became a port where a lot of the allied equipment came in.

20

A day or two after the landing another fella and I were walking down a road. One of the French civilians ran out and stopped us. He was very excited, waving his arms around, talking in French of course. Neither one of us understood French. He seemed quite upset and wanted us to come with him.

We didn't know what was going on, but we followed him around in back of the barn. In back of the barn was a dead paratrooper, who had been killed after he parachuted in.

This Frenchman kept saying, "Boom, boom."

He tried to make us understand, and we finally understood that the body had been booby-trapped by the Germans. We told him the best we could with sign language in addition to our very bad French that we'd learned out of the book they'd given us, that we would take care of it.

I went back to the battery and reported to my Battery Commander, Captain Paddock, that this paratrooper's body was lying back there and a Frenchman said that the body was booby-trapped.

Then I went back on my gun, working on the gun, firing etc. After a while they called over the telephone for me to report to the Captain again. I walked over to where he was and there were also a couple of engineers with a jeep.

Captain Paddock said, "Look, you go with these engineers and show them where that paratrooper is. They want to see if there is a booby-trap under that body. We don't want the grave registration guys coming along and getting blown up when they pick that body up."

So, I went back with those engineers in the jeep and showed them where the paratrooper was. They tied a long rope around the ankle of the body, got around in back of the barn, pulled on the rope and kind of slid the body along for about five or six feet. It turned out that it wasn't booby-trapped; it was a false alarm.

We had to be very, very careful because the Germans left a lot of booby-traps in all kinds of ways. We had a couple of fellas in my outfit that were killed with booby-traps.

The motor Sergeant in our battery found a German generator in a cave or a hole. I didn't see it, just heard about it. He went into this dugout and said,

"Hey, guys look what I found. I got a generator. I bet I can get this baby working."

He dragged the generator out of this dugout and checked it for gas, made sure it had gas in the tank. When he pulled the starter cord to start the thing up, it blew up and killed him. The generator had been booby-trapped.

We had another fella by the name of Marvin Chavis that came under fire while he was out on wire patrol. He jumped into an empty foxhole. The Germans had booby-trapped the foxhole and it blew up and killed him. Unfortunately, that was the same fella that was in charge of quarters when I first joined the Division. He was the one who had been so nice to me when I first came into the outfit. It really made me feel bad to hear that he had been killed.

There was also one that Ernie Pyle wrote about. This was up in the Hurtgen Forest. Ernie Pyle wrote that a Fourth Division soldier had his leg blown off with a mine. He was lying out in the middle of this clearing, but the medics couldn't get to him because the Germans had the field under fire. That night under the cover of darkness, the Germans came out to the fella. He was still conscious and they placed a pressure sensitive mine underneath his body. So that if he rolled off of it, or somebody picked him up, the mine would go off and either kill or wound them.

The soldier remained conscious all that night into the next morning. The aid men were able to get out to him the next morning. He had stayed conscious all this time so he could tell them,

"Hey, be careful, there is a mine under me."

The medics got the engineers out there, de-fused the mine and got the wounded man back to the hospital safely. That was an amazing story that Ernie Pyle had written about. He traveled quite a bit with our Division.

One night we were on the gun. We always kept three fellas on the gun at all times. The gunner, the loader and the number one man. The number one man set the elevation and pulled the lanyard. At nighttime, if we weren't actually firing, a lot the rest of the fellas could try to get a little sleep and three fellas would stay on the gun.

If we got a fire mission, as soon as we fired it would wake the rest of the crew up and they'd be able to help out.

This one night I happened to be on the gun and things were pretty quiet. We looked out and it was really dark. All at once the gas alarm went off. This was a funny sounding thing that would make a clacking noise and then the sentry hollered,

"Gas!"

Boy, this was the first time we had ever had that alarm. We all scrambled to get our gas masks on. We'd had a lot of training in using a gas mask, gas discipline. But, so far the Germans hadn't used gas in WWII although they'd used it very extensively in WWI.

We all had our gas masks that we carried with us at all times. We even had what they called, gas-proof fatigues. Our fatigues were impregnated with a material that would help to keep the gas from getting to your body and burning you. These fatigues were very uncomfortable to wear because they were real stiff and had an unpleasant odor. They stunk!

Any way, we were all ready for this stuff. When we heard that gas alarm go off we put our gas masks on and were sitting there not knowing what to expect.

Pretty soon, it started to get light. The dawn was coming. We could see this mist coming across this field that we were overlooking. There was a misty cloud coming across the field.

I thought, "Holy mackerel, here comes that gas."

When you test for gas you lift up your gas mask and take a little sniff. I did that a couple times and I couldn't smell anything. After a while it got daylight and the mist just cleared away. Here it was, just a morning mist! It turned out that the whole thing was a false alarm!

It seems that the supply truck had come up with gasoline in five-gallon cans, called Jerry cans. The driver had unloaded these gas cans on the edge of the field and then he hollered out, "Hey you guys, come get your gas!"

All one of the sentry's heard was, "gas". He hadn't heard the rest of the message.

He hollered, "Gas!"

That had started the alarm going. There was quite a panic going on for a little while. Fortunately we were all able to laugh about it later. To my knowledge, the Germans never did use gas in World War II.

After a few days in combat, we kind of settled into a bit of a routine. The Sergeant and I divided the gun crew up; we had about ten men in the gun crew. We each took half. I had four fellas with me and he had four with him. We made two gun crews with two shifts. We'd work the gun in shifts. You'd be on for four hours and off for four hours.

We kept the gun manned at all times with the gunner, #1 man and #2 man in the tank with the 2 ammunition handlers standing by. In case of an attack the whole crew would pitch in. When you were off the shift you could shave, take a nap, and get something to eat, or go back to the last village we came through, as long as you were back in time for your shift.

The assistant gunner and I were determined that we were going to get Lugers for souvenirs. I wanted a Luger in the worst way. When we were off shift we would walk down the road or across the fields to the last village we came through to see if we could find anybody that knew where a Luger was.

We had practiced our French out of this little book of phrases they had given us before the invasion. We practiced this one sentence.

"Where could we find a German pistol?"

This one time, Joe and I were just on the outskirts of a little town. We walked back through this village and on the way we saw a place where the German bicycle troops had parked their bikes.

The Germans had some of their troops mounted on bicycles so they could travel rapidly, as opposed to marching from one point to another. When they came up to a place where they were going to form a battle-line they'd park their bicycles and fight on foot.

They'd parked all these bicycles along the edge of a woods and the Americans came along and the Germans had to retreat and leave their bicycles there. The place had come under pretty heavy shellfire and the bicycles really took a beating. Some of them were lying in the tops of the trees where the shells had blown them. Others were in a mixed up pile, all broken up.

There were a few Frenchman going through this pile of bicycles. They were cannibalizing the things. They would take one that had a good seat and take the seat off. Then they'd find another frame that was pretty good and take that. Then find a couple of wheels that weren't all bent up and take them off and put them on the frame. The first thing you know they'd have a whole bicycle and they'd hop on the bicycle and ride away.

Two Frenchmen were working, going through this broken up pile of bicycles. We walked up to them, offered them each a cigarette and asked them in our broken French,

"Where can we find a German pistol?"

This one guy says, "Oh, oh oui, oui!"

He acted like he knew. He motioned for us to follow him. He took us off into the woods. Joe and I followed him into these woods on a little path that kept getting deeper and deeper into the woods. Finally we came out into a clearing where the Germans had set up their kitchen. Their kitchen wagon was still there. It looked almost like the canvas topped Conestoga wagons that the pioneers used to cross the prairies with. Of course, there were no horses; they were gone. But there was equipment lying all over the place.

One thing I can remember to this day is that the Germans had a big pot sitting out alongside of the kitchen wagon. In the pot sat a big cube of butter, that piece of butter must have been a foot square. In another part of this park, they had hand grenades strewn around. Some of the hand grenades had that little red dot on the cap that I mentioned earlier. Of course we didn't mess with any of those things.

We looked around there and couldn't find any pistol. But the Frenchman kept motioning for us to follow him some more. He took off going deeper and deeper into the woods. After we had gone about half to three-quarters of a mile into these woods, it was getting thicker and darker. I started to think,

"Hey, this is pretty foolish, for the two of us following this guy."

I could just picture us walking into an ambush with a couple of Germans sitting up around a curve with a machine gun trained on this trail. So I hollered to the guy,

"Hey, we're going back!"

When I stop to think of it now it was a very foolish thing to do for a lousy Luger. To get shot up because we followed some Frenchmen that for all we knew was a German collaborator.

We threatened him with our carbines and made the guy lead us back. We went back and that was our adventure for that day, looking for a Luger.

We had about four or five fellas in our Battery that came from Louisiana. They spoke Cajun French fluently, very fluently. They were a big help, they acted as interpreters when we had dealings with the French people.

We were set up in a gun position right along side of a little lane, a little dirt road. A couple of Frenchman came down this road. One was helping the other. When they got closer we saw that one fella had been shot through the knee. They were looking for medical assistance.

They were jabbering away and we didn't know what they were talking about. We went down to one of the other guns and got one of the Cajun's from Louisiana. He talked to the Frenchmen.

It seems that the Germans had rounded up about a dozen of these Frenchmen. They suspected them of being part of the resistance, the FFI, which is French Forces of the Interior. The Germans lined them up against a brick wall and shot them.

These fellas were in that group. One had gotten shot in the knee and the other fell down and pretended he was dead. The Germans had killed all the rest of them. When the Germans went away, they came down this lane to find help.

The little fella from our battery, we called him "Pistach" (which means little peanut in french,) and I took them down to the Battalion Aid Station and turned them over to Doc Willey to fix up the guy who had been shot.

They weren't really too upset, I was surprised. Here they had been almost executed by this patrol of Germans. They just acted like it was just one of the hazards of being in France at the time.

One night my crew was manning the gun when we got word back from the forward observer that it looked as though the Germans were preparing to attack. I woke up the rest of the gun section and just about that time we received orders to commence firing.

There were so many targets that we were firing steadily, as fast as we could throw the rounds into the gun. After what seemed like a long time of this steady firing our gun started to get so hot you couldn't place your hand on the barrel. When a 105 is fired there is quite a bit of recoil and there is a hydraulic system mounted on top of the barrel, which is filled with oil and this cushions the action when the barrel, or tube as we called it is returned to the forward position. The proper expression is "going back into battery".

Well, we had been firing so much and the gun was so hot that the oil got overheated and became just like water. The tube started slamming back into battery harder and harder with every round. After a while it was causing the whole tank to lurch forward so we finally had to call our gun out of action while the other three guns of the battery continued to fire. The battery commander radioed back to Ordinance and told them that we needed a new tube section immediately.

In the meanwhile the rest of the battery moved out to another position leaving our gun there along with a 50-caliber machine gun and crew to wait for the Ordinance truck. We were a little nervous being left all by ourselves but we soon heard this big truck coming and sure enough it was the fellows from Ordinance. They had a huge truck with a big frame on top of it with a hoist; hanging on the hoist was a whole new howitzer unit. I never saw a crew of men work so fast, they must have had that gun replaced in 10 minutes and then went tearing down the road back to their outfit.

We all said that they didn't like being so far forward. We put the machine gun crew aboard our tank and moved forward to the new gun position and joined the rest of the battery. By this time things had quieted down and we didn't do much firing for the rest of the night.

21

A few days after Joe and I had the adventure with the Frenchmen and the bicycles, we had a little bit of time off. It looked like we were going to be in a stable position for a few hours. At this time in the war we never knew how long we were going to be in a position because we kept advancing. Sometimes we'd move our guns two or three times a day. Other times we'd be in position for a day or two and then advance. We never knew how long we were going to be in one place. When we were off duty we couldn't leave the gun for long periods of time.

This one-day we had the opportunity to get away for a couple of hours. We walked back to a little village we had passed through. We wanted to go and check this village out, still looking for our souvenirs of course.

We came to a big farm; it was a typical dairy farm in Normandy. It had a stone wall that enclosed the house and the barns, with a courtyard in the center. The house made up one side of the courtyard; the stone wall would make up the other three sides, with the barn in back of the house. Everything was made of stone. It was a pretty big farm.

We came to the gate, the opening in the wall. In the courtyard there was an old man, a young boy and girl. The boy and girl were about twelve or thirteen years old. We went in, said hello and offered the old man a cigarette, trying to see if he knew where we could find a pistol. The boy could speak just a little bit of English, very little, but he could understand us and we could understand him.

After a lot of gestures he said. "Ah, oui, oui."

He knew where we could get a pistol. He pointed inside the house. We looked in the front window and could see that the Germans had been billeted there, the enlisted men had been on the ground floor. They had straw on the floor where they had been bedded down and there was a lot of equipment lying around. They had obviously left in a hurry.

The kid wanted me to go in the house with him. I told Joe to stay outside and keep an eye on things and I'd go and see what the kid had inside there.

So we went inside the house and looked around. There wasn't anything on the ground floor except straw and a few knapsacks lying over in the corner, nothing that I was really looking for. I couldn't see any pistols lying around.

He motioned for me to follow him up the stairs, so we went on upstairs and we went into this one room where you could see the officers had been living. It was a nice room that had a little table in the center of the room and the bed was over in one corner. On this table was a bottle of wine and a piece of sausage. You could see that the Germans must have jumped up and ran out, everything was in disorder.

Over in the corner was a leather holster with a pistol in it. The kid saw it first and he pointed it out to me.

He said, "Look there's one!"

Of course I was armed with my carbine and I said. "Well, pick it up."

He didn't want to pick it up. I didn't want to pick it up either because the Germans were very proficient with their booby-traps. You go in a strange place like that and pick up something and you could be standing there looking at a stump where your hand used to be.

I finally pointed my carbine at the kid and made him pick the pistol up. He picked it up and handed it to me and I stuck it in my pocket.

Then he opened the closet door and there was a couple of officers uniforms hanging there but I don't know what rank they were. There was also a pair of boots.

He wanted me to take one of the uniforms, but I didn't want a uniform because I had no place to put it. All I wanted was the pistol.

The tension kind of eased off a little bit once I saw the pistol wasn't booby-trapped. I gave him a D ration which was a very highly fortified chocolate bar with all kinds of vitamins. One of these bars was supposed to have enough calories to keep you going for one day.

To the French these chocolate bars were a real delicacy. We were talking back and forth and I didn't realize how long we'd been up there. All of a sudden I heard Joe hollering out in the courtyard.

"Yo, Ed! Yo, Ed!"

I thought he was in trouble of some sort so I ran down the hall. I had to go past a big window before I ran down the steps. The big window was right at the head of the stairs. Just as I started down the stairs the whole window was smashed to smithereens. I could hear the glass breaking in back of me, but by that time I was half way down the stairs. I never knew what broke the glass in that window, I often wondered whether someone had shot through the window or it had been weakened from the bombardment of the artillery and bombs.

I ran down the stairs and out into the courtyard and there was Joe with about ten Frenchmen lined up against the barn wall with their hands up in the air. He had his carbine on them.

He was yelling:

"Come on, come on get your hands up!"

When I came out he said, "Where have you been?"

I said, "I went upstairs with this kid and got a pistol up there. What are you doing sticking these guys up?"

He said, "Well, I thought something had happened to you. I was standing here talking to the old man and the girl and a couple of guys came around from one side of the barn. Two or three others came through the gate. First thing I knew there were a whole bunch of them standing around me talking in French. Of course, I don't know what they're talking about. Then I saw a couple of guys come around from the back of the barn with a piece of rope in their hands. I thought they had hung you and were coming after me! So, I put my gun on them, lined them up against the wall and started hollering for you."

I started to laugh. The kid had come down the stairs in back of me. He explained to us that these fellows were part of the Resistance. They all belonged to the FFI. This farm was the meeting place for the FFI and they were meeting there to go out on a patrol.

We gave them our cigarettes and Joe apologized for sticking them up and we had a big laugh about it.

The pistol turned out to be a .25 caliber automatic in a leather holster with a little pocket in the side for a magazine. It held about eight or nine rounds. The magazine was loaded, ready to go.

We went on back to the gun. I showed my souvenir to all the guys in the gun section.

I said, "I think I'll take this things apart and field strip it and clean it."

They said, "Hey don't do that around here. Go out in the middle of the field."

They were still afraid that it was booby-trapped. So I went out in the middle of the field and field stripped the pistol, nothing was wrong with it. I cleaned it up and that became my war souvenir.

Joe was kind of jealous because there was only one and I got it. The next day he found a pistol that they used to drop by parachute to the Frenchman for their uprising when the invasion came. It was a very crude pistol, but it would shoot. It was kind of an oddity. I don't know if he ever got his home or not, but I did manage to get my pistol home and still have it to this day. It is mounted on a plaque, hanging on the wall.

22

One night we moved into a new position in an apple orchard. We set the gun up and prepared for action. It started to rain lightly. We put a camouflage net over the tank so that it couldn't be spotted from the air. We had a big tarpaulin that we used in case of rain. We had big bows made of metal tubing that we'd put up on the tank and throw the camouflage net over. We put the tarp and then the camouflage net over the bows. Then we'd be sheltered from the rain a little bit.

At daybreak we had a chance to get a bite to eat. I'll never forget the date. It was June the 21st, 1944. We had been firing off and on and we were within range of Cherbourg. We were firing into Cherbourg at the time.

In back of my gun position was a little chapel, a church. It was a couple of hedgerows in back of us. It got to be around 11 AM; we'd been firing off and on.

All of a sudden the church bells started to ring. We thought, "Gee that's funny that the church bell would be ringing on a Wednesday." There weren't many civilians around.

The Captain called me on the telephone. All the gunners were hooked up with the Captain or the firing officer by telephone. The gunners wore head-sets and we had a throat mike so we could talk on the phone without having to hold anything with our hands. We had both hands free and could talk back and forth with the firing officer.

This particular day it was Captain Paddock. He called on the phone and said, "Corporal Kent, do you hear that church bell from your position?"

I said, "Yes Sir, we sure do. It's right in back of us."

He said, "Send a couple guys out there to check it out and see what it is."

I told a couple of the fellas to go on back and check it out. They were gone about five or ten minutes and then came back. The bell had stopped ringing by this time. It only rang a few times and then stopped.

They got over to the belfry and there was just the rope swinging. Someone had been ringing the bell but there was nobody around there.

I reported back to the Captain. I told him, "There wasn't anybody there."

He said, "Alright, have a couple guys keep an eye out there."

We didn't think too much of it, but it wasn't too long after that we had been firing, in fact we had a round in the gun when they gave me the order to hold fire and they were going to shift the guns to another target.

I was sitting in the gunner's seat, just looking over the top of the shield of the gun looking at the ground. I was listening on the headset for the change in deflection. As I did the ground right where I was looking erupted. An artillery round had landed directly in front of our gun.

I thought, "Wow, that was a pretty close one!"

Captain Paddock called me on the phone and asked.

"Is anybody hit over there?"

I said, "No, we're all okay."

He proceeded with the change of deflection. In the meanwhile my number one man, my machine gunner, lay back in the machine gun turret and said,

"Hey, that next one is going to be right in here!"

I said, "Nah, they can't hit us. We're just a little tank out in this big orchard."

Just at that instant Captain Paddock gave me the change of deflection and I reached up with my hand for the gun sight and that instant directly over our head they dropped an air burst. It just rained down on our gun, shrapnel flying all around.

A piece hit me in the arm; of course at that time you just go into shock. I knew I'd been hit, but I didn't know how badly. I kind of had a sick feeling in my stomach. I hadn't realized the shock it would be when you got hit like that.

The concussion of the burst knocked me down and it knocked me down into the driver's seat, only I was sitting in the driver's seat backwards. I was kind of stuck down in the driver's seat.

While I was stuck in this seat I was hollering for the Greek, my Sergeant.

"Yo Greek, Yo Greek! Come help us!"

He didn't come and I thought that was awfully strange, I knew that he would help me if he could. I heard this funny noise; a gurgling sound and I didn't know what it was.

We'd had a fella that had joined us the night before as a replacement. I was teaching him how to load the gun. He got hit right square in the knee. He jumped over the side of the tank and the hooks on his legging got caught on the camouflage net. He was swinging on the camouflage net. He couldn't get back in the tank and he couldn't get down to the ground. He was yelling,

"Help me!"

I got my trench knife out and reached over with my left hand and cut the camouflage net so he could get down on the ground and get into a hole.

The machine gunner that had been lying back in the machine gun turret looked awful. I thought he was dead. He had screamed the instant that we all got hit and he fell down across the breech of the gun and slid off onto the deck of the tank.

I learned later that he had gotten hit twice in the face, twice in the arm and twice in the leg. Boy he was bleeding all over the place!

I could tell that my arm was broken. I zipped down my jacket, I had a tanker jacket on and I stuck my arm in the jacket and zipped it up so it would support my arm.

Then I noticed that a piece of this hot shrapnel had gotten down in back of one of the ammunition racks. I kept the oily waste in there that you clean the gun with. The hot shrapnel had gotten on this oily waste and it was starting to burn.

We'd been firing all morning and we had powder bags lying on the rear deck. The rounds had seven little powder bags in them and sometimes we'd have to cut the charges if the firing officer didn't want the projectiles to over-shoot the target. As we removed the excess bags we would throw them in a pile on the rear deck. When we got the time we'd take the pile out into an open area and burn it.

I figured man, if that fire gets into that pile of powder bags we won't have to worry about anything else. I managed to get the waste out of there, it wasn't burning that bad but it would have been a catastrophe if we hadn't gotten it out.

Then I called over the telephone that we'd been hit and we were out of action. I was also calling for a medic.

Our medic came over, jumped up on the ladder welded to the side of the tank and looked in. His eyes looked like they were six inches across, they opened so wide! When he looked in there it must have been a scary scene.

Doviak was lying there on the floor of the tank, all covered with blood. By this time you could hardly stand up in there it was so slippery with his blood. It was a real mess.

The medic worked on Doviak first because he was hurt worse than I was. My assistant gunner Joe came up in the tank and I told him,

"Look, give me a shot of that morphine."

We had a little kit that every soldier had. It had a morphine surette so if you got wounded you could have your buddy give you a shot of this morphine or you could give yourself a shot.

It had started to hurt pretty bad by then so I asked him to give me a shot. He tore open my sleeve on my left arm and he was gingerly trying to stick this needle in, just trying to prick it. I said,

"For God's sake jam it in there!"

So he jammed it in all the way and it helped ease the pain a little bit.

Some of our gun crew took Doviak out and put him on a litter and then came up and dragged me over the side and laid me on a litter. At this time the Germans started throwing artillery rounds in all around us.

Everybody was diving into their foxholes and I couldn't get off the litter to get into my foxhole. It seemed like a long, long time, but the shelling finally stopped.

When Captain Paddock came over I asked him what had happened to the Greek? He told me he had been hit pretty badly. It seems that he was down in a foxhole sitting on a box getting his hair cut. We had a guy in our battery that used to cut hair.

The Greek had been sitting on this box and he had a parachute around his neck. The guy who was the barber used it for a barber's cloth. When the first round hit everybody dove in their foxhole. We couldn't of course because we were up on the gun and had to stay there to fire.

There was a little pause after the first round hit. The Greek must have stood up and looked out of his foxhole. When the second round went off he got hit right in the throat with a piece of shrapnel. That was the gurgling sound I had heard, the Greek breathing his last.

All together the Germans got five of us with that one round. They killed the Greek, got the three of us up in the tank and one other guy that was down on the ground. He had been lying in a slit trench and he got hit in the back.

It was a chaotic morning. Our tank was knocked out. A piece of the shrapnel had hit the engine and it wouldn't run. The other three tanks got the order to move out to a new position. They were really bringing the artillery in pretty hard on us.

In between the artillery rounds coming in the medics brought up a jeep, one that they put the litters on. They put Doviak and me on this litter-jeep.

I didn't know what happened to the kid that had gotten hit in the knee. I heard later that they had to cut his leg off but I never saw him again.

The medics took Doviak and me on this jeep to the Battalion Aid Station. The Battalion Aid Station was set up in an orchard. It was a big hole in the ground that had been dug and had a tarp over it. They would carry the guys in there and Doc Willey would patch them up and then they would move them out by ambulance back to the field hospital.

There was a lot of wounded coming in all at once. They laid me on the ground underneath a tree. There were a couple of guys along side of me lying in a row on these litters waiting to be taken in to where Doc Willey was.

First thing we knew the Germans started shelling this orchard! They were hitting the trees. The worst kind of artillery to be under was either a tree-burst or an airburst. If they hit the ground its not really too bad unless they hit real close to you because the force of the explosion and shrapnel goes up from the ground.

But when they have an airburst it just rains down and a tree-burst does the same thing.

The German artillery was hitting these trees and the shrapnel was flying all around the Battalion Aid Station. The guy on the litter next to me got hit and it killed him, he never lived to get in to see the doctor.

A couple of medics came and picked up my litter and took me in and Doc Willey patched up my arm. He put a big bandage on it, gave me another shot of morphine and made a sling for my arm. Then they laid me back outside.

After a while it got to be nighttime. They loaded me in an ambulance and we started back heading for the field hospital. By this time I had a couple shots of morphine and I was kind of passing out and coming to, passing out and coming to.

These ambulances didn't run all the way to the field hospital. They would only go so far and then they would meet another ambulance, transfer you and go right back to the battalion aid station and pick up more wounded and take them back to the collection point where the other ambulances would meet them.

I don't know how many ambulances I was in. It seemed that every time I opened my eyes I was in a different ambulance.

Finally we got to the field hospital. I must have been unconscious when we got there. I remember opening my eyes and I was on a litter. There were two guys carrying me and they were taking me into this big tent. I looked up at the guy who was carrying my head and he was a German soldier, in uniform. I looked at the guy at my feet and he was also a German!

I thought, "Holy mackerel! The Germans must have captured us!"

They took me into the tent, which was the operating room, and the two doctors had their masks and white surgical outfits on. I looked up at them and asked them,

"Are you guys Germans or Americans?"

He said, "Don't worry son, we're Americans. Those guys are prisoners we have working here carrying the wounded back and forth."

I was very relieved!

The two doctors were having a discussion. One wanted to cut my arm off and the other thought they could save it.

He said, "Why don't we just put a cast on it and send him back to England. I think we can save it."

The other doctor finally agreed. So they didn't bother to take the shrapnel out. They just put a cast on my right arm. I had passed out because they gave me some sodium pentathol. They had set my arm, because it had been broken just above the elbow.

23

When I woke up I was back in a big ward in the hospital tent. We used to call the male nurses ward boys. This ward boy came along and said,

"Oh, you're awake now?"

I said, "Yeah, where am I?"

He said, "You're in the field hospital and they are going to send you back to England."

I thought they were going to take me down to the channel and put me on a boat. But it turned out that they were going to fly us back. There were a lot of casualties that had to go back and we had to wait our turn. I guess I was in the field hospital for three or four days, it got kind of blurry.

This ward boy asked me, "Do you have any valuables that you want me to put in the safe?"

I had my pistol rigged up in a shoulder holster under my jacket, up under my armpit.

I said, "Yeah, I've got a watch and a pistol."

He said, "Well, give them to me and I'll put them in the safe."

I'd heard all kinds of stories about these guys, the ward boys in the hospital. You'd give them a pistol or something like that and you'd never see it again. But I had no choice, really. So I gave him my pistol and my watch.

Three or four days later when the doctor came in to check me out on his daily rounds, he told me they were going to fly me back to England that day.

The ward boy came in with this little bag and said,

"Here's your pistol and your watch."

He restored my faith in ward boys.

The medics put about three or four of us in another ambulance and took us down a little closer to the channel where there was an airstrip. It was where the American engineers had bulldozed a flat piece of land out and laid these metal strips to make a landing strip. There were a lot of fighter planes taking off and landing there.

I remember I was in a tent set up along side of the landing strip. We were in there all night, a bunch of us lying on the litters. The litters are only about two or three inches off the ground.

The next morning a C-47 landed and the crew loaded us on the plane and flew us back to England. It was very interesting when we took off in the C-47. The pilot banked out and made a big wide turn to gain altitude to head off across the channel.

The head of my litter was right near a window, so I could lie there and look out. When he banked around I could see the whole coast where the invasion had taken place. Boy, what a sight! There were all kinds of gliders stuck up at all angles in the hedge rows, airplanes that had been shot down lying all over the place, and burned out tanks and trucks. It was quite a memorable sight! It was real messy there after D-Day.

The flight across the channel was pretty uneventful. After the plane landed in England the medics put us on a train. The train took us to, Stratford on Avon to the 182nd General Hospital. That was the start of my long hospitalization.

When I was hit I thought that I would just go to a field hospital, my wound would heal up and I would be back with my gun battery in a few weeks! Little did I know that was the last time I would ever see any of those fellas. It always made me feel bad that I never had a chance to say "so-long" to any of them. These were guys that I had served with for three years. To leave them just like that made me feel sad. I always regretted that I didn't realize that was the last time I was going to see any of them. I also didn't know that was the end of my fighting days.

I've often wondered if the ringing of the bell in that church had anything to do with our gun being pin pointed the way it was. The first round that came in was right in front of us and the second was right over our heads. Of course, we'll never know if that was somebody signaling or attracting attention to our position. It was one of those mysteries of the war that we'll never know.

After I got home from the war my mother told me of a strange thing that happened to her. One day she didn't feel well and was lying on the sofa in our living room at home. She wasn't certain if she had fallen asleep or was just dozing, but she was startled to hear me call "MOTHER." She said that she *knew* something had happened to me. She was very upset, but she said that she also knew that I was still alive.

She was not at all surprised when she received a letter from me stating that I had been wounded, the letter arrived before the War Department sent her a telegram.

When we compared dates and times it proved to be the same day and approximately the time that I was wounded. Strange things happen!

24

After arriving at the 182nd General Hospital in Stratford on Avon we were unloaded from the train and taken to the ward that was to be my home for quite a while. The train-load of casualties that I was on was the first to arrive directly from the battle front at this hospital in England and it seemed to me that all of the personnel of the hospital were lined up to welcome us. I was still in the same set of fatigues that I had been wearing when we loaded on the landing craft before the invasion and needless to say I really needed to get cleaned up. After assigning me to my bunk the ward boy asked me if I would like to take a bath. I told him that I thought that would be a good idea so he took me into a big room with an old-fashioned bathtub sitting in the middle of the floor and said:

"I'll help you get bathed",

I was a little embarrassed to have someone give me a bath so I told him,

"That's 0. K. I can manage."

But he insisted because of the big cast on my arm. Seeing that he was determined to give me a bath I let him help me out of my clothes and then enjoyed the luxury of relaxing in a big tub of hot water. It was a little uncomfortable because I had to hang my right arm over the side of the tub because of the cast. It certainly felt good to get all cleaned up and put on a nice pair of pajamas.

In the field hospital in Normandy they didn't have the facilities for the casualties to get baths and have pajamas, but back in England we had all the luxuries that went with being in the hospital. After getting all cleaned up the ward boy took me back to the ward and told me that the doctor was going to come in and clean my wound.

When the doctor came in and looked at my arm he told the nurse:

"Get this man down to the x-ray room, take some pictures and then we'll get that piece of shrapnel out."

As soon as the x-rays were developed they wheeled me into the operating room and proceeded to sedate me. I asked the doctor if he would save the shrapnel for me and when I finally regained consciousness the piece of metal was on my bedside stand and I had a new, more comfortable cast on my arm.

This new cast had a large hole over the entry wound and a smaller hole over the place that the doctors had removed the shrapnel so that both wounds could be dressed. Also, unlike my first cast this one ended at my knuckles so that my fingers were exposed and I could use my hand in a very limited manner. It seemed that I could grasp things with the fingers of my right hand but I couldn't release them. I didn't think too much about it at the time because of the constriction of the cast, but after a few days I told the nurse that my fingers felt strange and were very numb.

The ward boys took me back to the cast room and with a pair of shears they enlarged the opening around my thumb, thinking that the circulation would return to my thumb and the knuckles of my right hand. No one knew at that time that the radial nerve had been severed. The radial nerve controls the action of a person's wrist and hand movements and if it is damaged or severed you cannot raise your wrist or fingers, a condition known as "Drop Wrist".

I assumed that now that the shrapnel had been removed and the upper arm bone had been set that it was just a matter of healing and resting and then eventually I could rejoin my outfit to continue with my part of the war. Little did I know that I was only beginning my long, long road to recovery.

Life in the hospital settled down to a predictable routine. I was one of the lucky ones that were able to get out of bed and walk around. It was a little easier than being forced to lie in bed with a leg wound or worse. Those of us that were ambulatory did what we could to help our comrades that were bed-ridden as much as we could. Since I could not use my right arm because of the heavy cast, I had to learn to do everything with my left hand.

The second day after I arrived at the hospital a Grey Lady came around and asked if I wanted her to write a letter for me. I really appreciated her offer and dictated a letter to my mother, which by the way, she received before she got the telegram sent by the War Dept. informing her that I had been wounded in action. After that I was determined that I wasn't going to depend on other people to write for me so I learned to write with my left hand. It was slow and laborious but I finally succeeded and did a pretty good job of eating, shaving and writing left handed.

25

The ward I was in had approximately 60 beds and they were filled nearly all the time. The patients kept coming and going as they improved, but as soon as a fellow going to the Rehabilitation Center emptied a bed there would be a new casualty to take his place. Consequently I met many interesting fellows and I'll tell you about a few of them.

At night after the ward boy turned out the lights it was sometimes very difficult to go to sleep so we would take turns telling our "War Stories". It would usually start off by someone calling out to the newest patient "Hey Joe, how did you get hit?" and that would start it off and one after another the guys would relate their adventures.

One of the fellows was a paratrooper who had his left hand all wrapped up in a big bandage. When he jumped into Normandy in the early morning hours of D-Day he'd lost his rifle when he hit the ground. He said it was the hardest landing that he had ever made. While he was looking around for his weapon in the dark a German soldier appeared and was getting ready to shoot him. Seeing that he didn't have a chance he put his hands up and said "0. K. I surrender". With that the German shot him through the ring finger of his left hand.

The Germans rounded up a few more paratroopers and proceeded to load them all in a truck to take them back for interrogation. One of the Germans was sitting on the tailgate of the truck guarding the prisoners as the truck was going down the road in the darkness. When my friend was captured they didn't search him very well and he still had his jump knife strapped to his boot. He told the trooper sitting next to him:

"Tell the others to follow me!"

And with that he drew his knife, stabbed the guard and pushed him out of the truck, then jumped out after him. Since the truck was moving at a fairly good clip the escaping American prisoners were all spread out along the road and he never did see any of them again. He hid out during the day and tried to work his way back to the American lines at night. He finally was picked up by a patrol of the 4th Division infantry after three days. In the meantime his hand had gotten badly infected and was about the size of a head of cabbage. After a short stay in the hospital he made a quick recovery and was soon on his way back to his outfit.

Another fellow had been a tank commander (a Sergeant). He had been riding with his head sticking out the hatch and holding on to the rim of the hatch when the tank came under enemy fire. The driver tried to take evasive action and backed under a tree. The tree limb slammed the hatch shut on the sergeant's hand and cut off four of his fingers. When the Colonel came around to pass out the Purple Hearts the fellow with the bad hand was embarrassed because he thought he wasn't entitled to one because he hadn't been shot. We all laughed and told him at least he was building up points toward his rotation.

Another character was asked how he got hit and he replied:

"I didn't get hit, I shot myself."

We were all astonished to hear this because he was an experienced soldier having participated in the landings in North Africa, Sicily and then Normandy.

Someone asked,

"How did an old soldier like you shoot yourself?"

He replied "Oh it wasn't an accident, I meant to do it."

He explained that he had been in combat in Africa, Sicily and Normandy and he got tired sleeping on the ground and eating C rations. So he thought a hospital stay would be a good rest. He told us that he asked his buddy to shoot him in the butt because he had heard it didn't hurt too much to get hit there, but his buddy refused. So he put his hand over the muzzle of his carbine and put a round through the palm of his hand. Fortunately for him, it missed all the bones and tendons, but it was serious enough to get him back to England where he got a chance to sleep in a clean bed and eat hot food for a short time.

We were all astonished that he would tell us what he did because it is a court martial offense to have a self-inflicted wound. I don't know what his official story was but he was with us for a short time and then sent to a Replacement Depot and I suppose finally wound up back in his old outfit.

One of my closest hospital friends was a fellow by the name of Mack Bush; He was assigned the bunk next to mine after I had been in the hospital for a couple of weeks. Mack was one of the Rangers who climbed the cliffs at Pointe Du Hoc on the morning of D-Day. His assignment was to climb a rope ladder to the top of the cliff and to help destroy the artillery pieces that our intelligence reported were there. This was a very important mission, as the guns would command both the Utah and Omaha beaches. Mack was the seventh man going up the rope ladder and the first one to reach the top. All the Rangers ahead were either shot off or fell off the ladder.

He said he was very lucky because there was a German machine gunner sweeping the edge of the cliff with machine gun fire. But when Mack stuck his head over the edge of the cliff the gunner was firing in the other direction. Mack rolled into a shell hole and engaged the machine gun with rifle fire.

After a rather fast and furious firefight, the Rangers took the position at the top of Pointe Du Hoc only to discover that the artillery pieces were not there at all. Later in the morning they discovered the battery of guns quite a ways back from where they had expected to find them. They took them under fire and destroyed them.

A few nights later Mack, armed with a B.A.R. (Browning Automatic Rifle) along with a couple of rifle-men, were manning a road block when they heard a motorcycle coming down the road. They knew there were no friendly troops out in front of them so as soon as they saw the motorcycle Mack opened fire with the B.A.R. It turned out to be a motorcycle with a sidecar attached. The driver was hit with the first burst of fire and the cycle turned over in the ditch killing the driver and the passenger in the sidecar. When the Rangers went over to check it out they found that the passenger had been carrying a leather valise in his lap. When they opened it up they found it full of French money. They presumed that it was a German paymaster on his way to pay the troops and the cycle driver had taken a wrong turn in the dark.

One of the Rangers said that this money probably wasn't any good so they were carelessly throwing it away, starting fires with it lighting their cigarettes with it etc. Mack thought to himself, "Hey, maybe this is real money." So he stuffed handfuls of it down his pant legs, he had no idea how much money he had.

A few days later in the battle for Cherbourg he was walking down a street when a German leaned out a second story window and shot him in the back of the head. He told me later

"It felt like somebody hit me with a baseball bat. I turned around and saw this guy leaning out the window, so I shot and knocked him out of the window. I started back down the street and fell right on my face in front of the Battalion Aid Station."

It seems the bullet entered the back of his head just below the rim of his helmet and came out his left cheek bone, passing through his inner ear in the process. When I knew him he was fine except for the fact that when he was in a small room or a hallway he would lose his balance. The bullet had affected his equilibrium. If he was out in the open he was fine.

After arriving at the hospital in England he gave a nurse one of the bills that he had stuffed in his pant legs and asked if she would check with the Finance Officer as to its' validity. She came back shortly and told him it was "Good as Gold". Mack had the French francs converted to English pounds, I never did find out exactly how much he brought back from Normandy with him but I do know that he didn't have to worry about spending money for a long time.

Mack and I bought a couple of used bicycles and we used to ride all over the countryside. However we weren't too fussy whether we had passes or not. The M.P.s didn't bother you much if they knew you were a hospital patient. With my big cast on my arm it was pretty obvious.

Mack would walk into a pub and buy drinks for the house. He would shout: "Drink up mates, this one is on the Germans!"

After a while Mack got very restless, he wanted to go back to his outfit but the doctors wouldn't give him clearance to ship out to a Replacement Depot. So one day he turned up missing. No one knew what happened to him, but in about a week we got word that the M.P.s had picked him up down at one of the Channel ports trying to get on a boat to get back to Normandy. I never saw or heard from him again. What a character!

The last "War Story" from the hospital in England that I'll tell you is about a fellow from my battalion. After Mack went A.W.O.L. another fellow was assigned his old bunk. I soon learned that he was from my Battalion, the 44th Field. He had been a Sergeant Pilot of one of our observation planes.

We had a couple of Piper Cubs attached to our Battalion that were used to spot targets for our guns. Some of the pilots were officers and others were non-commissioned officers. This fellow had been a Staff Sergeant until he flew under a bridge on a dare while we were training in England. Someone saw him fly under the bridge and got the number of the plane and reported it to the authorities. He was consequently busted back to a Private. Since he was a very competent pilot and mechanic his commanding officer kept him in the air wing as a mechanic, although he wasn't supposed to fly any more.

Since these planes flew so low and slow they were very tempting targets for the Germans. When the enemy troops saw these planes fly over their positions they knew there was a very good chance of coming under our artillery fire almost immediately. One of our spotter planes landed on a dirt road right next to our gun position. It looked like a sieve where the Germans had shot it full of holes. The pilots were a wild bunch; some of them would take up a whole box of hand grenades and try to throw them out the window at the enemy positions. One guy rigged up a couple of bazookas wired to the wing struts and would try to dive at the Germans and fire the bazookas at them.

One day the plane came back from a mission shot full of holes and my friend was assigned to repair it. After repairing the plane he decided to take it up and check it out since the regular pilot wasn't around. After taking off and checking out the plane he decided to fly over the lines just to see what they looked like. Unfortunately for him he flew over a German Anti-Aircraft gun and they shot him down. He crash-landed in a pasture between two hedgerows halfway between the German and American lines. He had gotten hit with a piece of shrapnel in the left elbow but was still able to get out of the wreckage and run for the safety of the hedgerow.

After he had been with us for about a week the new copy of Yank magazine came out and there was his picture on the cover of Yank magazine. The photograph showed him climbing on a C-47 preparing to be flown back to England. The picture showed him with his left arm in a sling and a big bandage wrapped around his head. We asked him,

"What was the matter with your head?"

He replied "Nothing, the photographer thought it would make a better picture so he wrapped my head up in a bandage, took the picture and then took off the bandage."

We all had a good laugh about that and he was quite the celebrity for a while. It wasn't every body that got their picture on the cover of Yank.

26

When I first arrived at the hospital in England the nurse would dress my wound every day through the hole that the doctors had left in the cast on my arm. This was a very painful procedure as she would take a long swab and dip the end in antiseptic solution and then proceed to run it all the way up inside my arm to clean out the wound. The pain was rather severe and I didn't look forward to this treatment, but the doctors told me that the wound had to heal from the inside out. It seemed like forever but it was probably only a couple of weeks but eventually the wound healed.

One day the ward boy took me to the x-ray room for a couple of pictures to see how the bone in my upper arm was healing. Shortly after that a couple of ward boys showed up with a wheel chair and said:

"Come on, we are going to change your cast."

I said: "I don't need a wheel chair, I can walk."

They replied, "No, we have to use the wheel chair."

So I climbed into the wheel chair and they pushed me down the hall to the cast room and proceeded to cut the cast off with a big pair of shears. My arm was very scrawny and weak after being in the cast, but it felt so good to have it off so I could give it a good scratch. Before I knew what was happening one of the ward boys grabbed me by the shoulders and held me while the other one grabbed my arm and started to bend it right where the break was. I started to holler,

"Hey, wait a minute-you're going to break my arm!"

One of them said: "Relax, it will be over in a minute."

And with that I could hear the bone snap. It seems that the x-ray showed that the bone wasn't set correctly. Instead of the ends being lined up they were lapped over one another and if it hadn't been re-set my arm would have been crooked. One of the fellows, that I thought was a ward boy, turned out to be an Orthopedic Doctor. Then he proceeded to set my arm correctly.

After putting a new cast on my arm they wheeled me back to my bed. I then realized why they needed the wheel chair because I was as limp as a dishrag after that ordeal.

27

I still had my souvenir pistol hidden away in my personal belongings and I was a little apprehensive of the possibility of someone finding it, especially since I had a full magazine of ammunition in it. One of the other patients had a Mauser pistol but no ammunition and since he was scheduled to be shipped out to the Replacement Depot and then back to combat I gave him the ammunition that I had. Both pistols were .25 caliber. He was glad to get my bullets, as that size ammunition was hard to find.

I don't think the commanding officer of the hospital would be too happy to find a loaded gun in my ditty bag, so I felt relieved to at least get rid of the ammunition. However, I was determined to get my pistol home.

The hospital had a public address system, with loud speakers in every ward. At times during the day one of the fellas volunteered as a disk jockey and played music over the PA system to bolster the patients' morale.

I had mentioned to a couple of the fellas that my birthday was coming up on July 14. On my birthday as I was lying on my bunk the disk jockey was playing music. I heard him announce that this song was dedicated to Ed Kent and he started playing Tommy Dorsey's "Song of India", which was my favorite song at that time. It was just a little thing, but it made me feel so good that my friends would remember my birthday. This was my twenty-first birthday.

After a couple of months we started getting Italian prisoners of war admitted to our ward. Most of them had been captured in North Africa and had been in England for quite a while; they were being treated for malaria. I could never understand why they were put in the same ward with wounded Americans, but no one seemed to be worried about their escaping.

A couple of our fellas spoke Italian, but none of the Italians could speak English so it was a little difficult to mingle with them. Once in a while we would play cards with them and by the time I was transferred to the Rehabilitation Center some of them knew a few words of English.

The people in England were very kind to the wounded American soldiers. The Red Cross would arrange for the ambulatory patients to spend a day with an English family, have dinner with them and get to know them.

I went to dinner at the home of an English family and had a very enjoyable time. They didn't have much to put on a dinner with because of the strict rationing but they were willing to share what they had with us. This English family had a son in the army that they hadn't seen for a couple of years. He had been fighting in North Africa and Italy. I hope that he made it home O.K.

My wounds were all healed and the bone in my upper arm had knitted together and the cast had been removed, but the doctors were very disappointed to find that I couldn't use my right hand. As hard as I tried I couldn't raise my wrist or my fingers the hand just hung limp. At first they thought I just needed physical therapy so I was transferred to a Rehabilitation Center, the 307th Station Hospital near Leamington Spa. This was quite a change from the hospital; I was assigned to a Quonset Hut that held about ten men. We lived in these huts, ate in a mess hall and pulled light duty and received medical treatment as necessary.

In my case this meant a lot of physical therapy, electro-therapy and Hydrotherapy. The physical therapy and Hydrotherapy were supposed to strengthen my muscles. The Electro-therapy was supposed to stimulate the nerves in my arm. Day after day I would work with all different types of equipment to loosen up and then strengthen my muscles and bones. I made good progress with the use of my arm; the elbow was working fine, but my hand was as limp as a dishrag.

The therapists were all young ladies and were very kind and patient with us. Some of the fellas would get disgusted and wouldn't even try to help themselves, but I was determined that I was going back to my outfit.

The Electro-therapy consisted of the application of a couple of electrodes on my arm and then an electric current was applied to stimulate the nerves. The therapist could control the strength of the electric current. There are certain nerve centers in your arm that when stimulated with electricity causes an involuntary movement of the muscles. The therapist would move the electrode to a certain spot on my forearm and hit the button and my wrist would jerk sideways. Then she would put it on another spot and hit the button and there was no response.

She said:

"Your wrist should kick up when I do that."

So she would crank up the electricity and do it again, no response. Finally she would really give it a jolt and there were still no results. This treatment went on for weeks but I made no progress.

The men that were assigned to the Rehabilitation Center were classified or graded according to their physical condition. Every week we had to go before a board of doctors that would review our charts and see how we were responding to the treatments. As I recall there were three classifications: A, B & C. Grade C meant that the patient needed quite a bit more treatment. Grade B meant that he was making progress and would shortly be moved up to Grade A. Grade A meant the patient would be in the next group to be transferred to the Replacement Depot on his way back to the front. If possible, they would try to send you back to your old outfit, but that wasn't always the case.

I met one Staff Sergeant who had been wounded five times and was going back into combat again. He didn't seem to be too concerned about it, most combat soldiers become rather fatalistic. He told me,

"Sooner or later my luck will run out, I just hope the war is over before it does."

Every Saturday morning all the patients at the Rehabilitation Center would be formed up for a parade and would pass in review before the commanding officer of the post and his guests. The purpose was to remind us that we were soldiers first and hospital patients second.

At this time the doctors had fitted me with a device called a Banjo Splint. It was a rather cumbersome thing that consisted of a cast on my forearm with a metal hoop fastened over my hand and attached to the hoop were five rubber bands with a little leather pocket on each of them that I could place my finger tips into. This device would keep my fingers extended since I couldn't extend them myself. It looked as though I was carrying a banjo, hence the name "Banjo Splint." The cast was split lengthwise with laces on it so that I could take it off to shower and to sleep, otherwise I was ordered to wear it all the time.

Well, this one Saturday we fell out and were formed up for our parade, it was all really very military with the band leading. I actually enjoyed it very much because we paraded with a band of Scot Pipers with a Drum Major in a tall fur cap and a long baton. They were all dressed in their kilts.

This particular day we had paraded down the Company Street and out onto the parade ground. We were passing in review and as I followed the command for "Eyes Right" I noticed the General look at me and then turn aside to say something to one of his aides. The next thing I knew this Lieutenant was marching alongside me with a notebook and asking me my name and serial number. I thought,

"Uh-Uh what did I do now?"

The next day I was ordered to report to Headquarters where the General told me that he was so impressed with my military bearing despite the Banjo Splint on my arm that he was putting a letter of commendation in my file. I still have a copy of that letter in my records at home. It was just a little thing but it made me feel good, because I always tried to be a good soldier.

Another time we were marching back to our Quonset huts after the parade and we passed a number of new fellows just coming in from the hospital with their barracks bags thrown over their shoulders. I noticed this one guy that was walking down the street ahead of us and I thought to myself,

"That guy walks just like Bo Willis".

We had a fellow in our battery that could never march properly, when he walked he would throw one foot out sideways and the Sgt. was always yelling at him. But I guess he couldn't help it. Anyway, when our column caught up to this fellow I looked over and sure enough it was Bo!

I couldn't fall out of formation, so I called out to him, gave him the number of my hut and told him to come down to see me when he could. He was the first person from my outfit that I had seen since I was wounded, which by this time must have been five months. After a while Bo came over to my hut and we had a nice visit. He gave me all the latest news about the outfit, who had been killed and who had been wounded. Bo had been shot in the foot and when I asked him how he got hit he said:

"Alfred shot me."

Alfred was another fellow in our battery; he and Bo were both truck drivers. "Why did Alfred shoot you?" I asked Bo.

He said: "Oh, he was cleaning his carbine and it went off and hit me in the foot."

Naturally I had no reason not to believe Bo, but a few months later I found out the truth. After I had been sent back to the states I was home from the hospital on convalescent furlough and a fellow named Lester Flitcraft had been sent home on rotation. Since he lived in Woodstown, a town rather close to my hometown, he stopped over to see me. In the course of our conversation I happened to mention the fact that I had run into Bo Willis in the Rehabilitation Center in England.

"Hey, how about Alfred shooting Bo Willis?" I asked.

Les said: "Alfred didn't shoot him, Bo shot himself. One cold morning Bo was sitting in the cab of his truck and the fellows around the area heard a shot. Then Bo fell out of the cab. He had shot himself in the foot. He claimed it was an accident, but now hearing that he told you that Alfred shot him it looks as though it might have been intentional."

Les and I both had a good laugh about Bo; he had always been sort of a "Sad Sack".

I mentioned self-inflicted wounds earlier. They weren't all that common, but I personally ran into two fellows with SIWs. I also heard stories about other guys that were so fed up with the living conditions we were forced to endure that they would mutilate themselves in order to get out of combat.

One story that I heard many times was that a guy would pull the pin on a hand grenade and stick his arm around the corner of a building. He'd hold the grenade in his hand and release the lever and blow his hand off. I never knew anyone that had actually seen that happen, but some men get so desperate that they will do anything. This is a court martial offense and if it were proven that a soldier shot or hurt himself to get out of combat the Army would deal very harshly with him. Not only is he showing cowardice, but also he is letting his comrades down.

As I mentioned before we had to appear before a board of doctors every week to be evaluated as to our fitness to return to duty. I had been in the hospital about 5 months by this time and it didn't seem that I was any closer to getting back to my outfit.

I thought that I would try to make something happen. The next time I was up before the board of doctors I told them that I would like to volunteer to be upgraded to Class A, ship out to the Replacement Depot and eventually rejoin my outfit. As soon as I said that the doctors (there were four or five of them on the board) all started to look at all my charts and records and confer amongst themselves.

Finally one of them said to me, "Hold your arms straight out in front of you."

My left arm and hand were fine but my right hand just drooped at the wrist.

He shouted, "Hold your right hand up!"

Of course as much as I strained I couldn't raise my hand.

He said: "What good would you be up there with your outfit?"

I had no answer to that question.

Turning to the other doctors he said; "This man should be sent to the Zone of the Interior, he needs an operation."

They curtly dismissed me soon after that and within a week I was on my way back to the States along with a large group of other patients that were too seriously wounded to return to their outfits.

28

A rumor went around that we were going to be flown home. We were all elated to hear that! It seemed that there had been a change in plans and instead of flying back to the States we were flown to Glasgow, Scotland. There we were to catch a ship for the voyage home.

The flight from England to Scotland was one of the worst experiences of the war for me. We were loaded on a C-47 transport plane which had no seats, just benches along each side of the fuselage. On the plane I was on all the patients were ambulatory, so there was no need for litters.

The crew consisted of a pilot, co-pilot, a couple of nurses and also a Sgt. who seemed to be in charge of loading us on the plane. We had no sooner taken off than the air became so rough it was impossible to stand, all we could do was hold on.

It wasn't too long before the fellows started to get sick and that was contagious. Before we landed just about everyone was sick, including the nurses. The farther we flew, the rougher it got, we thought the flight would never end but finally we landed at an airport near Glasgow.

This was a huge movement of casualties as plane after plane kept landing. There was a large hospital right at the edge of the airport and we were told to go into a big hangar to be assigned our wards. The ward that we were assigned depended on the type of wound we had. We were formed up into long lines and were to be interviewed by a doctor who would assign us to our various wards.

I was standing in back of a fellow who had a wound similar to mine (he had been shot through the elbow and couldn't move his arm.) We had met in the previous hospital and had become friends. After quite a wait we finally got up to the desk where the doctor was seated and he asked my friend what was his problem. Ray gave him his envelope of records and told him,

"I have a bad arm."

So the doctor replied.

"Report to ward upper L."

So being next in line, I stepped up and said:

"I'd like to be in upper L too, Sir."

He said: "What's your problem?"

"I have a nerve injury of my right arm" I answered.

Without even looking at my medical records he said:

"Report to Ward A."

I suppose that he was so rushed that it really didn't register what I had said or he didn't hear me correctly over all the noise of the gang that was in that hangar (there were hundreds of us) but anyway I knew better than to question an officer's decision. So off I went to Ward A. I had all my belongings in a small barracks bag over my shoulder and I followed the rest of the crowd all looking for the wards to which we were assigned.

I didn't see Ray so I figured he had already found his ward. I passed building after building, all labeled with signs indicating the letter of the wards. Other fellows would fall out of the line and go to their assigned wards until finally I was all by myself. I still hadn't seen Ward A. Finally, I saw a single story building down at the end of the path with a high barbed wire fence around it and an M. P. standing at the gate.

I asked him, "Where could I find Ward A?"

He said "This is it, did they send you down here by yourself?"

"Sure, isn't that O.K.?" I replied.

He said: "You better go in and see the nurse."

So I walked inside the building and went up to the nurse's desk and told her I was checking in.

She said: "Where are your papers?"

I said: "I don't know, I guess the doctor kept them."

She took me into the ward and assigned me a bunk. There I unpacked my toilet articles, arranged my bedside cabinet and started to look around at my fellow ward-mates. There didn't seem to be too many fellows in the ward and it was very quiet, which I thought was strange because usually there is a lot of talking back and forth. Every body seemed to keep to them selves. After chow, which was brought in on trays I read a couple of magazines and took a shower and went to bed since I was rather tired after that terrible plane ride.

In the middle of the night a guy screaming and running up and down the space between the beds jolted me out of a sound sleep. The nurses were trying to calm him down. I didn't think too much of this behavior because some of the patients that I had been with before had been pretty jumpy.

In the 182nd General Hospital in England one of the fellows hid under the bed every time a plane went over. He spent a lot of time under his bed because we were very close to an English airfield. After a while he got used to it and was O.K.

I figured this was just a guy having a nightmare so I rolled over and went back to sleep.

The next day I happened to look out the window and saw some of the fellows that I had flown in with the day before walking off the hospital grounds and going to the bus stop, So I went to the nurses desk and said:

"I'd like to get a pass to go into town."

"No passes." She said.

I said: "What do you mean, no passes, I see other guys going out the gate."

She replied, "No passes for this ward."

I asked "Why not?"

She said: "You know this is the Psycho ward."

I said: "WHAT? I'M NOT PSYCHO, I WAS WOUNDED!"

Most of the soldiers treated for battle fatigue didn't have a scratch. I proceeded to roll up my sleeve and show her the scars on my arm and told her about the radial nerve being severed.

I said: "Look at my medical records, I was only in combat 15 days. How in hell could I be psycho?"

She said: "We don't know where your records are."

I shouted, "That's just great! You better find them quick because I'm not going to spend another night in this ward."

Within a couple of hours my medical records had been found and I was transferred to Ward Upper L. Ray and I laughed about it later but it wasn't funny to me at the time.

The next day I got a pass to go into Glasgow. As I recall I didn't do much more than walk around the city looking at the sights. It didn't appear any different than a city in England; the double-decker buses and the small taxis were the same.

In the course of my walk I came upon a photographers shop where you could have your photograph taken dressed in an authentic Scottish kilt complete with the purse in front and the dagger in the stocking. I have always regretted that I didn't take advantage of that opportunity but I probably didn't have enough money at the time.

Most of the time that I was in the army I didn't have one penny to rub against another. After a while I caught the bus back to the hospital. If I had known we were shipping out so soon I would probably have stayed longer in town, as that was the only chance I got to see that part of Scotland.

29

In a day or two we were told to pack up our personal belongings and get ready to move out. The ambulatory patients were loaded on buses and the litter cases were moved by ambulance. We were all taken down to the dock area where we loaded aboard the Ile de France, which was one of the biggest luxury liners at that time. It wasn't very luxurious then because it had been pressed into service as a troop ship. However, the accommodations were much better than on the Capetown Castle that we had come across to England on.

This time I stayed in a stateroom, with four other soldiers, instead of down in the hold with the whole battery. The five of us thought we were living like kings and couldn't quite believe that we were really heading home! We also realized that we were probably going to make it through the war alive after all.

Because of the ship's speed we didn't travel in convoy, but came across alone. When I questioned a sailor about that he assured me that no U-boat could catch us and we didn't have anything to worry about. It was rather an enjoyable trip. We had a following sea most of the time and I used to like to walk to the stern and look back at the wake. It was just like riding an elevator, the seas were so large they would lift the stern up and the prop would come out of the water, vibrate and then the stern would drop almost out from under me. It was quite a thrill.

I believe our journey only took five days, on the second or third day we heard over the radio that the Germans had broken through the lines in the Argonne Forest. This was the beginning of the Battle of the Bulge.

All of the patients aboard were thinking of their friends in their old outfits and wondering how they were making out. I didn't know where the Fourth Division was at that time, but I found out later that they were fighting to save Luxembourg. They were successful; our division held back the Germans and prevented them from taking the city.

We learned that our ship was headed for Boston and that we would be sent to the hospital at Camp Edwards, Massachusetts. In addition to the hospital patients the ship was carrying many soldiers returning home on rotation and many USO performers who had been entertaining the troops overseas. We were all returning back to the States.

When we finally tied up at the dock in Boston harbor they announced over the public address system that everyone would have to go through customs. I hadn't expected that; it meant that I stood a good chance of losing my souvenir pistol. For months I had been hiding the pistol and worrying about being caught with it in the hospital. I was determined that if I had to lay out my things for inspection, I would throw the pistol overboard. It was hidden in the bottom of a little ditty bag that the Red Cross had given me for my toilet articles which I carried in my hand when I went up on deck.

When we got up on deck and started to line up for the customs officer they announced over the P.A. "All hospital patients will proceed to the gangway and prepare to disembark, everyone else will have to go through customs."

What a relief! When we got to the gangway and looked down at the dock there must have been a hundred army ambulances lined up to take us to the hospital at Camp Edwards.

One of the fellows had his upper body in a cast, with his arm sticking out in an awkward position. He was storming up and down the deck in a rage. He claimed he could see his parents' house from the deck of the ship but the officer in charge wouldn't let him go home to see his parents. Instead he would have to get on the ambulance along with the rest of us. I imagine his parents came to the hospital as soon as he called them.

We were allowed to make a telephone call home as soon as we got settled in at the hospital. Needless to say my dad and mother were thrilled to hear from me; they knew that I was on my way home but hadn't known exactly when.

30

The Station Hospital at Camp Edwards was the collecting point for all the casualties coming back from the European Theatre of Operations. The patients disembarked at Boston and then were taken to Camp Edwards. After an evaluation was made by the medical staff the patients were shipped to the hospital nearest their home where they could receive the treatment that they required.

We arrived at the hospital just before Christmas 1944 and on Christmas Eve a group of school children from the nearby schools came in and went from ward to ward singing Christmas Carols. It was rather an emotional experience to hear the old familiar carols and to realize that we were finally back in our own country.

In a couple of days the orders were posted on the bulletin board as to our final destinations. I was delighted to see that I was going to be shipped to Thomas M. England General Hospital in Atlantic City. I couldn't believe my luck to be sent so close to home for my surgery and treatments.

After a day or so, a group of us were loaded on a train and proceeded to Atlantic City. The government had taken over a number of the big hotels in Atlantic City and transformed them into hospitals and convalescent centers. The Hotel Haddon Hall was a fully equipped modern military hospital that specialized in amputations and neurosurgery. Before the war it was one of the most luxurious hotels on the beachfront and it still had some of the amenities left from the pre-war days. The lounges were very comfortable and well furnished and to soldiers used to life over-seas in the field it looked like paradise. This is now the Resorts Hotel and Casino.

I was assigned a room on the 9th floor over-looking the ocean and the ward boy who was on our floor told me that it would have cost $100 a night in peace time. I had to laugh because I didn't make that much in a month.

The room that I was assigned to was, to me, the height of luxury. There were only two beds in the room and after being in barracks and hospital wards with 50 or 60 other people that seemed great. We had a private bath and in the tub there were faucets for hot or cold fresh water and a set of faucets for hot or cold salt water, which I had never seen before.

One of the first things I did after I had settled in to my new home was telephone my parents and tell them the good news that I was right down in Atlantic City, which was only about 45 miles from home.

Within a couple of days they drove down to the hospital to see me. We had a joyous reunion and one of the first things that I did was to give Dad the German pistol that I had so furtively hidden all those months.

31

The patients that were physically able were given furloughs to go home and visit their friends and families before starting their surgery and convalescent procedures. I enjoyed being home for a while since I hadn't been home for a couple of years; but most all of my friends were away in the service so there wasn't much to do.

After my furlough was up I returned to the hospital to find that I now had a roommate. His name was Jim Baker and turned out to be quite a character. Jim had been a member of the 3rd Infantry Division and had landed in Southern France as a rifleman. One night he was out on a combat patrol and their squad was ambushed by a large group of Germans. In the fire fight that followed Jim was hit in the left forearm with a burst of machine gun fire. He lost 5 or 6 inches of bone, which the doctors replaced with a metal plate, but the nerves of his arm had been cut so he had an injury similar to mine. Jim and I were both scheduled for operations on the same day.

After a few days of medical evaluation and tests I was prepared for surgery and early one morning they took me to the operating room and proceeded to repair the severed nerve in my arm. The surgeon explained to me that the nerve is like a rubber band and when it is cut it snaps in both directions. So he would have to make a long incision on my forearm, reach up and grab one end of the nerve and reach down, grab the other end and pull them together and sew the ends together. He told me it would take a long time to heal, but with a lot of therapy I could probably regain most of the use of my hand.

The operation lasted for about three and a half-hours. I was conscious the whole time because the surgeon needed me to move my arm at times so that he could see the tendons and muscles working. It wasn't too painful because they gave me a local anesthetic and the nurses put up a screen so that I couldn't see the surgeon. Every so often he would ask me to straighten my arm or bend my elbow and then ask how I was doing.

After what seemed like an eternity he was finally finished and they took me back to my room. I passed Jim in the hall; he was on the way in as I was on the way out. We were both being pushed along on gurneys.

So there I was with my arm back in a cast once more. Hopefully this would be the last cast I would have to wear.

After the nurse and ward boy got me back in bed and left with the gurney I got out of bed and walked down the hall to the pay phone. I called Mother and told her that I had been operated on (we didn't have phones in any of the rooms but there was a pay phone on every floor). As I was headed back to my room a nurse saw me and really bawled me out because I was supposed to remain in bed for 24 hours after the surgery.

Jim had been on the operating table even longer than I had. When they brought him back to the room he wasn't feeling too well, but he recovered quickly. His left arm was in a cast and sling so we were a matched pair, with my right arm in a cast and sling.

After another day passed, Jim and I were allowed to go to the lounges and even get passes to go out on the boardwalk. It wasn't much fun walking on the boardwalk because it was wintertime and all the stores were closed up. On weekends we would both get passes to go to my parents house in Hurffville. Since he lived in Connecticut and couldn't get home easily I took him home with me to enjoy Mother's cooking (although the meals at the hospital were excellent).

When we were at the hospital we ate in the dining room, which was a huge place filled with long tables and we ate cafeteria style. The food was very good and we had many things to choose from. The patients that were not able to carry their trays (fellows in wheel chairs or amputees) would have someone assigned to help them; every one was so kind and courteous to the patients.

It was sad to see so many young fellows with missing hands or feet. Seeing them made me realize just how lucky I was. It seemed that the morale of the amputees was so good that it inspired the other fellows who had all their limbs.

When Jim and I were home I tried driving my Dads' car and found I could handle it well, even though my arm was in the cast. Because of gas rationing we couldn't travel very far but at least we were able to visit my brother Frank. He would take us out partying.

My Mother didn't care too much for Jim, she thought he was a bad influence on me. She didn't realize that we were just two soldiers celebrating our safe return from the war.

My Dad had cut down a couple of tall lombardy poplar trees that had grown too tall along side of his driveway and the trunks had to be cut up and hauled away. Jim and I volunteered to cut them, as we needed the exercise. Back in those days nobody knew what a chain saw was, everything was done by hand. It must have looked strange to a passerby to see two soldiers each with an arm in a cast at each end of a two-man saw. We laughed about that later but at the time we didn't think anything of it. Jim and I enjoyed having something useful to do.

32

After a period of time the cast was removed from my arm and my long series of treatments began. In the mornings, after straightening up the room and eating breakfast I had a series of appointments to keep with different therapists. One was Hydra-therapy where my arm was immersed in a tub of warm water that was being circulated, similar to a small Jacuzzi. After a period of time the therapist would massage my arm and try to help me regain my range of motion.

Then I would go to another office for Electro-therapy, which consisted of the therapist attaching electrodes to my arm and trying to stimulate the nerves with electric currents. Then I would go to another office for Physical therapy where the therapist would assign me to work a number of machines designed to strengthen my muscles. It was a long and sometimes painful process but gradually, little by little, I was making progress.

After a couple of months of these treatments I was sent to the gymnasium for exercise classes. I liked this part best of all. On the second floor of the hospital overlooking the boardwalk was a large solarium with glass windows all across the front. This had been converted into a gymnasium where the patients were given instructions in exercises and games to strengthen their particular disabilities. Many of the patients had recently been fitted with artificial legs, so there were many walk-ways with railings on each side where they could practice walking without the danger of falling.

As the seasons changed and the weather became warmer another fringe benefit was the fact that we could watch the people walking on the boardwalk out the windows of the gymnasium. You could tell the quality of the young female passersby by the quantity of wolf whistles you heard.

In the afternoons, if we didn't have any therapy appointments, we were more or less on our own. We could go down to the lounge and read or play cards or board games. When the weather got warmer we could get a pass to go out on the beach or the boardwalk. All of the personnel at the hospital and the many volunteers were so kind to the patients. We were still subject to Army discipline but they really went out of their way to make life as pleasant as possible for us.

One of the friends that I met in the hospital was a fellow by the name of Joe Martinovitch. Joe was a native of Czechoslovakia and had come to this country just before the war broke out. He was drafted and sent back to Europe to fight.

He had been shot through the thigh and the bullet severed the nerve in his leg. He couldn't raise his left foot up; they called that condition "drop foot" just as they called mine "drop wrist". Naturally he had to use crutches until the doctors could repair the damage to his nerve. After a while they fitted him with a contraption that was strapped to the calf of his leg. It had a spring under his shoe that would kick his foot up when he took a step. It gave him a distinctive walk, but at least he didn't have to use the crutches.

One day while he was still on crutches and Jim and I were still wearing our casts, Joe, Jim and I went over to the Steel Pier. We wandered around the pier and went to a couple of movies and then stood on the side-lines watching the people dancing to one of the Big Bands that was playing there at the time. Years later my wife, Carolyn, told me that she was at the Steel Pier that day and noticed two soldiers with their arms in casts and another on crutches. Little did she know that she was looking at her future husband! We didn't actually meet until months later.

Shortly after this the doctors decided to remove the cast from my arm. However, my arm had been in the cast so long that my elbow was locked and it was impossible to straighten my arm. The doctors told me not to worry, that it would gradually loosen up. I still had to carry my arm in a sling, but it was a relief to get rid of that heavy cast.

33

One day I was told to get my things together as they were transferring me to the Hotel Traymore which was right down the boardwalk a few blocks. It had been transformed into a Rehabilitation Center and was essentially the same as Haddon Hall except for the operating rooms. It was a lovely old hotel and was once one of the finest hotels in Atlantic City. But has since been torn down to make way for a casino.

One afternoon I was sitting in the lounge leafing through a magazine when I looked up to see what I thought was a ghost. Walking across the lounge was Walter Doviak, the fellow that was in the tank with me the day we were hit back in Normandy. He was the man that pulled the lanyard at my command and also served as machine-gunner. I assumed that he was dead, I hadn't heard differently. He had been so badly wounded that I naturally assumed him dead. He had been hit with six pieces of shrapnel, twice in the face, twice in the arm and twice in the leg. The doctors had done a good job on him and he looked pretty good. He was waiting to be discharged and he must have left soon after our meeting as I never saw him again.

It was rather hard for me to travel back and forth to my parents' home in Hurffville when I got a pass because there was no direct bus service. I used to hitch-hike quite a bit but that wasn't too dependable, although it was easy for a service man to get a ride in those days. I started thinking about getting a car but with the gas rationing that wasn't too practical.

One day my father told me of a fellow that had a motorcycle for sale, it was advertised on the bulletin board at the shipyard, where my Dad worked. I gave the man a call and fell in love with the cycle as soon as I saw it. I had never ridden a motorcycle in my life, but I bought it from him and practiced on the back roads. It was a military model Indian Scout that had been modified and repainted. It was perfect for me to travel back and forth from the hospital to home, as it was so easy on gas. I rented space in a parking garage right next to the Traymore and that worked out very well. I could be home in about an hour after leaving the hospital so I spent every weekend at home.

Life at the Traymore was just about the same as back at the hospital, with the same therapy every day but they were more lenient with passes. The weather was very pleasant and we could put on our trunks and spend the afternoons on the beach, if we wished. There was a private entrance to the hotel under the board-walk that opened right out onto the beach

I was progressing so well physically that I was given a 30-day convalescent fur-lough. The first week that I was home I thoroughly enjoyed myself just taking it easy and relaxing in my mother's hammock in the back yard. But after that, time started hanging heavily on my hands. All my boy-hood friends were in the service and were off fighting the war and I missed the company of soldiers because most of the civilians that I talked to did not understand some of my views of things. Being in combat changes your perspective.

When my furlough was up I was glad to get back to the Hotel Traymore, as I was getting bored. After a few days back I had a number of tests to re-evaluate my condition. Then I was handed a 60 day convalescent furlough.

This time I was determined to do something productive. Morris Nursery had an ad in the paper advertising for a truck driver. I called Harry Morris and explained that I could drive O.K., but was still in the Army as a patient and that I was still getting my strength back. He was desperate for help and hired me. It was an interesting job, I got to travel around the countryside of South Jersey, deliver-ing evergreen trees and shrubs and getting good, healthful exercise in the bargain. By the time my furlough was up I was in pretty good shape.

Back in May, when we received word that the war in Europe had ended every-one in the hospital was elated. About six weeks later I came back to my room to find that I had a new roommate. I can't remember his name but he was a Ser-geant and had been shot through the shoulder.

I asked him "What happened, did you get hit with the last bullet fired in the war?"

He replied "No, the war had just ended and my outfit was pulling occupation duty. We still carried weapons when we went into town because it was still dan-gerous. I had a P38 (a new model German pistol) that I carried in a shoulder hol-ster. I had just got back to the barracks off of pass and I took off the gun and threw it on my bunk."

The kid in the bunk next to mine had just arrived from the states and he said, "Oh Boy, is that a German pistol? Can I look at it?"

I said: "O.K., but be careful, it's loaded."

"He pulled the gun out of the holster and BAM shot me in the shoulder. I said GODAMMIT I TOLD YOU IT WAS LOADED. So here I am."

He was only with me for a couple of days but he had an interesting story.

34

One evening in August I was home on furlough and decided to go to a place called the "Dancette" in Oaklyn. I parked my motorcycle outside the place, went in and stood and watched the dancers. Most of the fellows were in uniform. I watched for a while and then started looking over the girls looking for a dance partner. I spotted a blonde across the room and it must have been love at first sight for me. I asked her for a dance and she and I danced most of the rest of the night together because I wouldn't let her go. Carolyn and I have now been married 56 years.

One day when I was in the Rehabilitation Center I was told to report to the Occupational Therapy room. This was a big room equipped with all kinds of machines to exercise different parts of the body. For example, there was a machine that looked like a stationary bike but it was connected to a jig saw so that the operator supplied the power to the jig saw while exercising his legs. The idea was to exercise the disabled portion of the body while doing something productive.

The therapist asked me what my problem was. After I told her, she suggested that I try chip carving. I didn't even know what she was talking about but she was very informative, got me the carving knives and the material and showed me the basics. This was good exercise for my hand and it wasn't as boring as just plain exercising. I made bookends for my mother and a couple of wooden toys for my niece.

After I was discharged from the Army I never thought about chip carving for over 50 years. One year Carolyn gave me a carving kit and instruction book for Christmas. Now it is one of my favorite hobbies and I've made many gifts for my family. My daughters both have some of my chip carving plates and boxes displayed in their homes. I often think back to that therapist, she would be proud of the fact that she taught me something useful.

Around the middle of October I got the good news that I was soon to be discharged from the U.S.Army. I rode my motorcycle home and left it there and hitchhiked back to Atlantic City. After a few days of final tests and misplaced files I was finally given my Honorable Discharge. I called my mother and made arrangements for her to pick me up at the train station in Haddonfield.

On the train heading home I fell to thinking that I had been in the Army three years ten months and seven days; fifteen days of combat and sixteen months in the hospital. As we pulled in to the station in Haddonfield I looked out the window and saw Mother waiting for me on the platform and I knew that my Great Adventure to Normandy and Back was over.

Ed Kent—June 2000

0-595-27314-9

edKww@pSHift.Com

edkwwzepshift.com

Printed in the United States
77170LV00003B/190-198